Praise for
Waves of Change

As someone who also lived through the Nashville floods of 2010, *Waves of Change* describes well what it was like in the aftermath of those very stressful days on the physical, emotional, mental, and relational health of those who lived through it. This is a must read for those flood survivors, but also for those who have lived through any natural disaster so that they can better understand their reactions and responses, and not feel that they are alone.

~ Sue Foster, MA, LMFT
Co-Author, *Finding Your Way After the Suicide of Someone You Love*

As sojourners on the road of human experience, we all face a lifetime of changes, some of which may appear to be impossible to overcome. *Waves of Change* is about people adjusting and responding to, and learning from the changes needed to recover from the aftermath of a natural disaster. This is an important body of work for those who have or will survive such devastation and the heroic people dedicated to help restore balance to their shattered lives.

~ Burt Winer, Ph.D., MBA, LMFT
President and CEO, Institute of Advanced Studies

Waves of Change

Waves of Change

How Surviving Tennessee's Thousand-Year Flood
Changed the Lives of a Survivor,
a Rescue Professional, and a Family Grief Counselor

by
Pamala Hernandez-Kaufman, LMFT,
MJ Plaster,
and Dr. Melissa Riley

Copyright © 2013
Waves of Change LLC
All rights reserved.

ISBN: 1489586237
ISBN-13: 978-1489586230

DEDICATION

To my children, you have given me strength, hope and purpose, have brought healing to the broken places, and have taught me that love truly does cover a multitude of sins. To Nichelle Christiana, my first born; Ryan William, my only son; Brianne Aubrey, my middle child; Alysse Kierstin, my baby of the family for many years; and Angelina Faith, my adopted gift, I will always love each of you best. B.A.T.W.

To my husband, Don, your kindness, generosity, and selflessness beckon me to be more and more the person God wants me to be. You graciously accept the late hours and late arrivals that accompany my work. Thank you for loving me just the way I am without judgment or ridicule.

To Mom and Dad, thank you for adopting me and giving me the life I had. You weren't with me long in this world, but I learned so much in the few short years. I think you would be happy with the person I am today.

To the many faithful friends I have been blessed to have through the years, you cause my heart to overflow with gratitude. It would be a lonely, difficult journey without you. Kimmy, I'll see you in Heaven one day.

To my mentor and friend, Burt, thank you for your steadfast leadership and guidance. You took over where my father left off; you make the world feel safe.

To my Titus women Sharon Kay, Julie, and Zena, you believed in me when I didn't and taught me what being a Christian woman really meant. I learned by listening to you and even more so by watching. I want to be just like you when I grow up.

To the many, many clients I have had the privilege of knowing, thank you for inviting this wounded healer into your innermost selves. You allow me to fulfill my calling as a psychotherapist: "The Lord has anointed me to bind up the broken-hearted, proclaim freedom for the captives and release from darkness... comfort those who mourn, and provide for those who grieve, giving them beauty for ashes... the oil of gladness instead of mourning, and a garment of praise instead of a spirit of despair." (Isaiah 61:1-3)

Finally, to my Lord and Savior, Yeshua, thank you for leaving the ninety-nine to search for the one who was lost—me. You are forever my Rock and Shelter through life's many Waves of Change.

~ Pam

How can I thank you, my rescuers, who plucked me from the raging waters! I don't know who you are, but I do know you are angels sent by God to save me.

To my parents and Yiayia who raised me to just get over it, pick myself up, and get on with it. May your memories be eternal. You are dearly missed but always in my heart.

To Miss Fluff, my fur-baby and another inspiration for this book.

To my neighbor Sheila and her family who provided immediate comfort and shelter.

To the Coutras/Arnold families, I will never forget your many kindnesses, for caring for my girlie girls and me, for giving us a long-term home when we had none, and for entrusting Georgie to my care.

My heartfelt thanks to Kathy (my sister from another mother), Richard, Mary, Carole and Terry, Jude and Don, all my friends and neighbors, and my parents' friends who kept checking in on me and never left my side.

To my cousin Joanie for giving me inspiration and for prodding me to keep on keeping on like she always does. Thanks for helping me laugh my way through yet another crisis.

To Alfonso for rebuilding my home.

To all my neighbors in Section X who braved the flood as troopers, especially my next-door neighbors on both sides and the neighbors in my immediate vicinity around the pool. I couldn't ask for better neighbors.

Special thanks to Holy Trinity Greek Orthodox Church, UMCOR, We Are Home, Garth Brooks for the many concerts on our behalf, and my fellow Nashvillians who answered the call of their fellow citizens. Thanks to Mayor Karl Dean who gave us the benefit of the doubt in his handling of the immediate aftermath of the flood and who fought to bring resources to us.

Thanks to Cindy and Damon for the gift of my precious Zorba the Cat, and to Danny who takes care of my four-legged family—and me.

Thanks to everyone at City Limits for giving me a respite when I needed one and allowing me to occupy space in my "office away from home" for hours on end.

Thanks to all the unnamed for your generosity and kindnesses. This book is dedicated to you for all you have given so selflessly to help me through my waves of change.

~ MJ

Thank you to my family (Alice, Pat, Allison, and Shawn and quadrupeds Stormy, Maggie, and Jo-Jo) and to each of my friends. All of you have made me who I am and who I continue to become. To the emergency response workers across Tennessee who risked their lives in the floodwaters saving countless others. Their stories of courage and perseverance need to be told. To the civilian rescuers who risked everything to save their neighbors. To my dear friend Elizabeth and her husband Brian for missing your wedding due to the flood. You know it was serious here if I missed that much free beer. YSR. To Anita, Melvin, and Dennis who led the State CCP program and made it an integral part of Tennessee's response to federal disasters. For all of the members of the Tennessee Recovery Project across the state who earnestly and tirelessly worked to touch the lives of tens of thousands of disaster survivors in the floods and tornadoes of 2010, 2011, and 2012. To the incredible VOADs that participated in the 2010 recovery work and to the thousands of volunteers who came to Tennessee from across the United States to help us recover. For the survivors, victims and responders of the 2010 flooding in Tennessee. Your courage, resiliency and hope will forevermore be carried forward.

*The Creator of the Heavens sent us down in His image
to walk upon the earth and reap all of its pleasures.
It is as a result of this that we are at play in the fields of the Lord.
When the journey is over and we have collected all that we can from the earth,
we begin our ascent back to Heaven and back to our Creator.
Though we are able to pass this way but once, it is what we make of that
passing that determines the character of person that is within us.
Our experiences are all that we can take with us on our ascent to eternity; we
carry no money or hold material objects.
The more chances we take to experience all that our Creator has given us, the
more enriched we will be when we return to His gates and
He asks us what it is that we have learned.*

~ Melissa

To all who have and all who will be affected by a disaster, our hearts go out to you, and our thoughts and prayers are with you. This book is for you. We look forward to hearing from you and sharing experiences, frustrations, and triumphs at waves-of-change.net.

~ MJ, Melissa, and Pam

CONTENTS

Vessel of Hope	iii

PART I – Shock!

Where's Miss Fluff?	3
What Now?	7
It Never Rains in Southern California	11
It's Just Rain	15
It's Raining Cats, Dogs, and Horses	19
Finding a New Normal in the Land of Grits and Grease	25
What? Another New Normal?	31
Comes the Dawn	34
Zero Degrees of Separation	39

PART II – MJ, the Survivor

The Road to Hell… Is Paved with Good Intentions?	45
Welcome to the FSA	50
The Long and Winding Road Home	55

Home at Last	61
Settling In	65
The Pause that Refreshes? Not!	71
Pay It Forward	78

PART III – Melissa, the Rescue Professional and Crisis Counselor

Heart the CCP	85
Santa, the Tooth Fairy, and the Easter Bunny	90
Heart Connections	95
SHHH! Best Kept Secret	98
What Stops the Hurt?	102
R & R: Rest and Renewal for the Caregiver	105

PART IV – Pam, the Family Grief Counselor

Come Hell AND High Water… But Not Necessarily in That Order	111
Happy New Year?	113
Building Bridges over Troubled Waters	116
Let's Talk Shop	119

The Three R's of Recovery	121
Undressing Stress – What Is It? What Does It Do?	123
Addressing Stress	127
Come On! Lighten Up a Little!	131
How Many A's in Anti-Stress? Eight!	134

PART V – Hope Springs Eternal

Hope, Resiliency, and Courage	138
When the Student Is Ready… The Teacher Will Appear	143
Lessons Learned	159
Moving Forward	168
Appendix	170

ACKNOWLEDGMENTS

Many thanks to Judith Fitzsimmons for editing a large portion of the book and for doing it with such humor and grace. Her innate ability to ferret out the fatal flaw always amazes. Judi, we look forward to abusing you again in the near future. And, from MJ, thanks for your support and humor during the flood. You provided bright little breaks from the daily grind! May I never have the occasion to repay that exact favor.

VESSEL OF HOPE

~ Kathy Budslick

My life was lost and rescued that day in May,
a forced cleansing of all that I hold dear.
The cruelty and unpredictability of nature
usually read only in the headlines.
Where is the handbook for grief?
Faith slowly restored,
as I stare into the eyes of perfect strangers.
Kind hearts heal even the deepest of wounds.
Strength prevails only after the waves of change.

PART I

SHOCK!

WHERE'S MISS FLUFF?

"Where's my cat? WHERE'S MISS FLUFF!" Those were the first words out of my mouth as I struggled aboard the canoe that rescued me from the grips of Nashville's Thousand-Year Flood and took me to safety early on the morning of May 2, 2010. Moments before, I had dropped Miss Fluff from the second story of my condo to the waiting arms of one of my rescuers. I had held her close, kissed her good-bye, and told her I'd see her on the other side.

I barely had time to move my three cats to safety on the second floor before the water started pouring in my front and back doors. My front door is a few feet from the retaining pond that catches the overflow from the Harpeth River, so mine was one of the first condos to flood. It wasn't long before the first puddles of water appeared, just as I was heading back upstairs with litter boxes, food, and water for the cats. By the time I got the cats settled, the trickle of water had turned into an avalanche and was making its way up the staircase. The flickers of light had extinguished into an eerie darkness as the electricity gave in to the rising floodwater.

I made one more quick trip downstairs and ran around like a crazy woman unplugging everything in sight. (Why didn't I think to turn off the circuit breakers?) I gave a second's thought to the irony of unplugging the washer in the middle of the spin cycle as my world was spinning out of control, grabbed a few documents from the safe, and high-tailed it back upstairs to relative safety, or at least to dry land. Then panic gripped me. My only thought was survival and how to accomplish it. I called a neighbor from my cell phone and asked her if we were going to die.

"No," she replied.

With that settled, I tried to figure out how Katrina survivors had climbed to their roofs—just in case things got dire here. I gave up; it didn't occur to me that they had slashed their way through the roof with pickaxes. (Note to self: buy a pickaxe immediately.) I decided that rescue was our only option, and I turned my attention to finding someone to rescue us. I opened the window, and ducking in and out between lightning strikes, I waved frantically and yelled, "Hello? HELLO!"

Within a few minutes, and what felt like hours, a voice answered back, "We're here to rescue you."

"Oh my GOD! I don't know who you people are, but you must be angels sent from God. You have to save my cats," I answered. "I have three."

"We can only take one," replied the woman. "Throw the cat, and I'll catch it."

I knew immediately that my recently deceased mother's year-old, girlie-girl sister kittens, Fifi and Fiona, would have the best chance of surviving in place, so I reluctantly chose to leave them behind. My older Norwegian forest cat had won the lottery—she would make it to safety that day, and I'd pray for the best for the little ones.

"Are you sure you'll catch her? I don't want her to drown."

"We do this all the time. Just throw her down."

I grabbed Miss Fluff and threw her to the woman, who actually caught her.

"Now it's your turn," the man commanded.

"Are you CRAZY? You want me to jump from up here?"

"We get that a lot. Trust me, we do this all the time," said the woman.

Trust her? To catch me as I rocket into a canoe from the second floor? "Well, you're not doing it with me," I said.

"Then you'll have to go downstairs and swim out to the canoe."

"No problem," I yelled as I darted for the stairs, feeling like a traitor for leaving the girlie girls behind and wondering just who in their right mind would actually jump. I was taken aback to find neck-deep water creeping halfway up the staircase and sloshing through the downstairs. Fortunately, I didn't stop to think what might be in that water. My wet jeans weighed me down, but I managed to make it into the office where I flung open the window, wrestled with the screen, wondered for a split second what to do with the screen, and then tossed it out into the water. I floated up to the windowsill, fought against water rushing in through the open window, and swam a few feet to the canoe where the two rescuers hoisted me to safety. I didn't think twice about swimming in the midst of an electrical storm until I was inside the canoe.

"Where's my cat? WHERE'S MISS FLUFF," I pleaded as I looked around for Miss Fluff when I fell into the canoe. "We have to find her!"

"I don't know. We have too many other people to rescue to stop and look for her, and we have to get you back to land—before the lightning gets any closer," said the woman.

Even as I sobbed, I knew the rescuers had plenty of work ahead of them to bring the remaining residents to safety, and of course, they didn't have time to look for a cat. I got that. I'm a former TWA flight attendant—from a time (Dark Ages) when flying around the world was an adventure, not a living hell since 9/11—where "safety first," not "YOU, the terrorist with an extra ounce of toothpaste, STOP," was our version of "Semper Fi."

I realized immediately that the woman had let go of Miss Fluff to help me into the canoe, something I probably could not have done alone without capsizing it. In retrospect, I know that instinct would have driven me to do the exact same thing. It's a rescuer's instinct, and that instinct saves lives. It was my instinct all those years at the airline, and it is my instinct even today. It was drilled into me, it's an integral part of who I am, and it probably has a lot to do with how I survived the flood and the aftermath.

As we approached the main road and the man helped me out of the canoe, I turned to him and thanked him for saving my life. I was in such a state of shock at the time that I didn't fully comprehend the magnitude of his heroic and kind act until later. Almost as an afterthought I asked, "What now?"

WHAT NOW?

"What now? I don't know," my rescuer said. "We have people to rescue, and you're safe now. Just make your way to the main road, and you'll figure it out."

As I walked the few feet to the main road, I knew he was right. I was safe—and alone, more alone than I'd ever been in my life. That was just one of the many thoughts darting through my head like greased lightning—so many thoughts, so few spare brain cycles left to process them!

As I waded through the water to cross the street, my mind raced through the scenarios I might have faced if my parents were alive. How would I have gotten them to safety? How would I have enticed my mother into water over her head? How would I have had handled my dad's belligerence, knowing that he would have had a better way—all of this when seconds can make the difference between life and death. As much as I needed family at this moment, it may sound strange, but I was oddly thankful my parents were gone. I suspected all of us might have drowned if I had tried to get them to safety.

After crossing the street, I turned back and looked toward the condo. I couldn't see it because the condos on the main road blocked the view, but I could see that most of Section X was under feet of water—many feet of water. As the water rushed down Sawyer Brown Road, I remember thinking, "So, *that's* what 'flash flood' means!"

I was blissfully unaware that one resident in my section had drowned in her unit and that a husband and wife from a neighboring section had drowned in their car. I was unaware of anything beyond my own little sphere, and I wouldn't learn much about the outside world for the next 12 hours. For all I knew, the whole city was underwater—or not. Who knew? I wondered how many of my neighbors and other Nashvillians were still stranded, left to contemplate their fate, or worse. All I knew with certainty was that I had failed Miss Fluff after nursing her back from death's door the past few months, and I felt derelict as a once-responsible pet guardian. Having nearly drowned in Puerto Vallarta on vacation, I knew the terror she must have felt, and I wanted to scream at the top of my lungs. Oh wait; I had already done that when I had gotten into the canoe.

I was soaking wet, so there was no pressing need to come in out of the rain or to give more than a passing thought to the downpour pummeling my body, except for the obvious—the lightning. The immediate need was to communicate with the outside world, the world beyond River Plantation. I pulled my cell phone out of my purse, which was stuffed like a weeklong airline carry-on with every necessity I could think to throw in it before hurling it down to the canoe.

Cell phone service was spotty, but I got a few calls through to my brother and friends to let them know I had been rescued. Fighting back sobs, the tone of those calls was harried and terse, because I knew I could lose the connection at any moment.

River Plantation is a very large condominium complex with 11 sections. Sections VIII and IX are located on higher ground just across the street from Sections X and XI. The neighbors in Section VIII and IX had already jumped into action, opening their clubhouses to us and gathering towels, clothes, blankets, blow dryers, hot coffee, soft drinks, food, and pet supplies. (The irony of pet supplies did not escape me.) By the time I arrived at the Section IX clubhouse, many of my neighbors were already there. It was a homecoming each time someone walked through the door, and our Section IX neighbors treated us like royalty.

The Section X resident "cat lady" was ushering in her brood of cats, each comfortable in its own carrier. She offered her sympathies for my loss and then lectured me about leaving my two kittens behind. "How could you," she inquired.

Wow, just WOW! I had killed one cat today, and now I had this near stranger reminding me that I had abandoned two more to fend for themselves while I sat here and drank hot, steaming coffee. "What kind of person am I," I wondered.

Once I was settled among my neighbors, I alternated between moments of hysteria over losing Miss Fluff and moments of calm where I was thankful to be alive. I wasn't ready to think about anything beyond the present moment. We spent much of the day welcoming rescued neighbors and helping them settle into this cocoon of warmth and safety. There were plenty of dry clothes to go around, and that was the first order of the day, our first luxury, after contacting people who otherwise would be left to wonder about our fate.

Word spread quickly that rowboat crews, canoe crews, and others had used Facebook and Twitter to organize civilian rescues all over town to supplement the city rescue efforts. We marveled at how swiftly Nashville had come together to take care of her own. Nashvillians didn't wait for any higher authorities to get organized and direct traffic. They rose to the occasion to help their fellow citizens—in true Volunteer-State spirit. And it didn't stop there. We later learned that grocery stores and restaurants that had lost electricity had fired up their grills, smokers, and gas ovens to feed anyone they could find and to hand out perishables rather than let the food spoil.

It didn't take long before the conversation and mood inside the clubhouse shifted to "what now?" What would our next move be? At this point, we all agreed that our next move was to find immediate quarters and to deal with the next steps as the situation unfolded. This may sound obvious, but we had just lost everything, not to mention the fact that we had just cheated death. We could only handle bite-size increments of reality.

That night and for the next few nights, I gratefully accepted the hospitality of my neighbor's daughter and son-in-law. They lived nearby, high on a hill. The first thing we did was to gather around the television where we learned the extent of the damage, which was far beyond our wildest imagination—mind-boggling. Few areas in town were spared. Opryland, the Titan stadium, and downtown Nashville were all underwater. Bellevue, our area of town, was one of the hardest hit, and from the aerial shots on TV, we could see that almost the entire area was underwater. More than half the state was submerged. We sat in silence and shared a surreal moment as reality finally began to seep in.

Later that night, I got a call through to my TWA friend and former flying partner in New Hampshire. Carole and her husband had been trying to reach me all day, and she was relieved to hear from me. After mentioning that she had spotted my actual condo on a Nashville TV station's website stream, using the clubhouse and pool as her point of reference, she asked, "What now?"

"Darned if I know," I responded. There would be plenty of time to figure it out in the coming days, weeks, months, and years.

IT NEVER RAINS IN SOUTHERN CALIFORNIA

In his 1970's No. 1 hit, singer-songwriter Albert Hammond told us, "It never rains in Southern California." This would explain why I could not comprehend what was happening that weekend—the weekend of the 2010 Tennessee flood.

I AM a Southern Californian (until the year of the flood, that is). I remember pondering at the time of the flood these three questions: 1) what am I doing here; 2) why did God bring us here; and 3) how could I get back home to sunny Orange County where this kind of craziness doesn't happen. Earthquakes, yes; tornadoes and floods, NEVER.

I will never forget that weekend. It rained Friday night, Saturday day, Saturday night, Sunday morning, Sunday day, and Sunday night. Not just normal rain—this was loud, pounding, merciless RAIN: rain that didn't stop; rain that turned the beautiful greenbelt behind our home into a lake; rain that threatened to enter our home within an inch.

I remember thinking about Noah and feeling as though I had never fully appreciated him or his ark—until now. I remember asking God why he had brought us here for this appointed time in history. Why now? Why here? This place called Nashville WAS my new home—not that I had asked for a new home, not that it felt like home either. I felt like a visitor, a foreigner, a stranger in a strange land. I had only moved here three weeks prior to the flood and those were not the best three weeks I had ever had. A month earlier, I had packed up my entire life and moved it far away from everyone and everything I had known and loved. I had driven across the country with two dogs, two kids, one cat, and one husband (not necessarily in that seating order in the vehicles) in just over three days.

It had been three terrible weeks of uncomfortable change and strange firsts. I prided myself in being a survivor. I had survived my first tornado warning, where I was gently reminded by a kind neighbor to "get out of the doorway and into a tornado closet." (I quickly learned that earthquake preparedness had little value in tornado country.) I had survived being told by my daughter's brand new school that she had lice and had treated her hair, my hair, and our home for lice, not once, not twice, but three times. I had survived two thunder and lightning storms, complete with full power outages—no phone, no TV, no cable, no computer. I had survived having my car broken into while ever so briefly parked in what I thought was a "nice neighborhood" and had subsequently driven windowless in 20 degree weather for 15 freezing miles home. I had managed to survive the stress-inducing trauma of studying for and taking another state psychotherapy-licensing exam. Apparently, Tennessee didn't care that I had one from California. I had survived the loneliness and isolation of living in the unfamiliar, crying myself to sleep every night, and being GPS dependent for any trips past the front yard. And now this?! Let's just say, it wasn't my best spring of record!

I questioned why my husband had to be away on business, why he always had to be away on business when stuff likes this happened. Then, I remembered. That's why we were in Tennessee in the first place—his business! His company had announced only six months prior that they were closing operations in California and moving to Nashville. My husband Don had to choose between uprooting a family of objectors over being jobless; given the state of the economy, his choice clearly had merit.

In the six months before our move, I had said good-bye to hundreds of psychotherapy clients, hundreds of family members, friends and acquaintances, two children, two grandchildren, and my beloved church family (not to mention my favorite California spots—the beach and In-N-Out Burger! Like most everything in my life, the last few days in California had been confusing. I had celebrated my 10-year wedding anniversary with a renewal of vows ceremony, which doubled as a farewell event. And just three days later, I had celebrated my last Easter Sunday in California. How's that for bittersweet! And what is it with the number three?

So there I was in my new rental "home" the morning of May 2, 2010—cold, scared, and alone—no friends, no church, no electrical power, no money, no nuthin', just my wet pets, my two kids, and me. And I had one question, "What in the heck is happening?" I paced, I pondered, and I prayed. "Lord, help me protect my kids and my pets."

It was about then I heard a knock on the door. There he was, Rick, that same wonderful neighbor who had helped me through the first tornado watch of my life. This time he didn't tell me to get in the closet. This time he told me to get OUT of the house. "Take your SUV," he said. "I think you can get it out of here, but the water's rising fast. Go now! Get to higher ground."

I did what he said. The kids, the dogs, the cat, and I were all drenched and freezing, but the lot of us crammed into the car. Somewhere in the midst of plodding along through the torrential downpour with zero visibility, making our way through the "river" that used to be our street, it occurred to me that I had no idea which way higher ground was. Was it to the left past the school or to the right past that little market? I had forgotten to ask neighbor Rick. I opted for left and proceeded to crawl along the main highway unable to see more than a few inches ahead of me. The brakes seemed hesitant and unreliable. I felt about the same.

I will never forget what I saw whenever there was a nanosecond of visibility. Everywhere was water, to the left, to the right, straight ahead, behind—nothing but water. And the water appeared to have swallowed entire churches, homes, and cars. A river raged all around. Fallen trees blocked the road and floating debris raced by. It seemed like we drove forever looking, searching for a place of safety. Then, out of the corner of my eye, I saw it—Green Hills Mall—Good name…considering the circumstances! Maybe it was a sign! I turned into the parking lot not knowing if anything would be open, not knowing if it would be safe there after all.

I shouted to my son, "Try the main entrance!" It was open. We poured in and so did the water. There we stayed for the rest of the day awaiting clearance to go home, uncertain whether there would be a home to go home *to*. It seemed like an eternity, but in reality, it was probably about eight hours later that we heard most of the homes in our subdivision were safe to return to, so we slowly made our way back. All I could think to ask to no one in particular was, "What's next? What now?"

IT'S JUST RAIN

It was supposed to rain. A lot. No big deal. It was just rain. I've always found rain boring. This wasn't the tornadic weather that always promised big rescue, big response, and big adrenalin. It was just rain. Who knew that plain old rain would change my life in ways I could never have imagined? Who knew it would seemingly never stop falling? Who knew that as a first responder, I was about to embark on a response that would last years? This would not be the adrenalin-filled day or weeklong tornado response and recovery. No! This would be different.

This time I would not be returning to my safe, insulated little world in a week or two. This time, the adrenalin and emotional odyssey would span years. It would change the face of my hometown along with 65 other Tennessee counties. This was to become known as the Thousand-Year Flood, and I just happened to co-exist during this particular time and place in history. It has been an amazing learning experience. At the same time, I would wish it upon no one for these lessons have not come easily. It was just supposed to rain.

It's Just Rain – Melissa

The first inkling I had that this rain would be anything but boring was Saturday night, May 1, 2010. The phone rang. It was the animal shelter in Wilson County. They were flooding, and they needed us to rescue the animals before the water reached them. I am the rescue coordinator for the Wilson County Disaster Animal Response Team (DART). I called the Wilson Emergency Management Agency (WEMA) to let them know what we had been asked to do and to request a boat from their water rescue team. I was told that they had no boats to spare; all boats were out on human rescues, and they would get to us when they could, but that wasn't likely. Mental note: not boring rain. This rain demanded attention, my attention. I responded by leading a water rescue that dark, drenched night. I put my gear in my vehicle, grabbed my keys, set the GPS, and started toward my destination.

Water was everywhere; it seemed to engulf everything. Places that had never been wet before, were. It even saturated my mind, flooding it with thoughts and questions. Would we be too late? Would the risk of rescue outweigh the benefit? Would we find a boat that we could use? Would the evacuation be successful? Would we have to watch animals helplessly drown if the risk outweighed the benefit? How many? Too many unanswered questions!

I arrived to find a moving current in front of the building and 88 dogs and cats to evacuate. There's no way to sugar coat it—I was terrified! Over two decades of emergency response experience had taught me to put aside that terror and focus on the here and now. Here I was with a borrowed boat, I had two other certified water-rescuers, and one shelter employee. It felt like we were understaffed, but we began our rescue mission anyway. As we began moving by foot pulling a small johnboat through unknown areas with live electricity running to the buildings, the operation teetered right on the edge of risk outweighing benefit. Just inside the margin of safety, we proceeded.

We decided to take the largest dogs first and then the cats. There was a method to our madness; in a worst-case scenario, the cats inside the building could climb to higher ground a lot easier than the dogs could. We had only enough life jackets for four dogs, so with one rescuer in the boat and with four dogs held by their life jacket handles, we proceeded. The rest of us waded through chest-deep waters while guiding the boat. You do the math—that's a lot of trips.

Any break in protocol in a rescue effort of this magnitude jeopardizes the entire operation. When life and death hang in the balance, there is no room for error. I absolutely refused to lose anyone on my watch, animals included. I'm certain, then, that you can understand my fury when a shelter employee broke protocol and appeared at the front door of the building after having taken a back route alone through the water. We had to spend an extra trip taking her back to the staging area by boat. It's absolutely imperative that everyone work as a team during a crisis!

Three hours later, we had evacuated all 88 animals without incident. Not one dog snapped at us, and not one cat tried to scratch us. I think they understood we were their only lifeline.

As we unloaded the last cat, to our utter disbelief, we discovered the animals had been placed inside a building in the half-flooded parking lot. Hello, it was still raining! We thought they had been taken to a temporary shelter at the Wilson County Fairgrounds. Unbelievable! There they sat in a half-flooded building. We could not leave the animals in a half-flooded area with more rain on the way! We had no choice but to repeat the entire rescue operation and complete a second evacuation of the traumatized, frightened animals to the fairgrounds.

Hours and hours later, as I drove home just past dawn the next morning, an uneasy feeling washed over me, a dreadful feeling that this was anything but " plain old rain." This feeling would prove correct. I would come to hate this flood as much as any disaster I had already survived. I was a tornado survivor as an infant, during the 1974 super outbreak, and again in 1997 when I lost my apartment complex to a tornado. Every disaster is devastating in its own right. However, after my experiences in the Thousand-Year Flood, I will never view rain as boring again.

IT'S RAINING CATS, DOGS, AND HORSES

Monday came—day three. Rescues were still in progress across the state of Tennessee. I was reminded why Tennessee is known as the Volunteer State. Local emergency resources were maxed out rescuing people from the floodwaters, and without hesitation, civilians, church groups, and local media jumped right in and joined in the rescue effort.

Animal rescue organizations coordinated via Facebook to locate animals in distress. My group of volunteers also coordinated via Facebook with animal rescue organizations to find out where animals needed the most help. We received word of animals facing imminent death, and 10 of us responded to the call making our way to the Opryland Hotel area. When we arrived, we met up with the owner of a boat dealership, and we learned of several dogs on land that would flood soon and a horse trapped on an "island." We sent the people without technical rescue experience to rescue the dogs that were on land. Two volunteers and I teamed up with boat owners who knew how to navigate floodwaters, and we set out on the equine rescue operation.

We found the horse, indeed isolated on a small bit of high ground in the middle of what was now part of the rapidly running Cumberland River, which had long since overflowed its banks. The Cumberland is the main river that flows through Nashville, and it was flowing fast, breaking debris loose from homes in large subdivisions. Guardrails, fences, and the like swept past us.

The horse was about three-quarters of a mile away. To reach him, we had to move perpendicular to the current for about a half mile. We couldn't see the underwater terrain, but if the propeller became entangled in any debris, it would prevent us from maneuvering. By the time we were a quarter mile from the horse, we could finally see him.

There was no time to waste. If the water rose any higher, he would be knocked off the island and swept downstream. A high-ranking Metro police chief assured us that the Corps of Engineers was finished releasing water for the day. Secure in the knowledge that the water level wouldn't rise any further, we attempted a rescue.

We approached the horse cautiously because we had no idea if he was used to human contact or the extent of his trauma. My friend Anne, who had worked animal rescues with me, was with me; and I trusted her with my life. I also had another member of the police department, Margie, who worked tirelessly with us on her day off to help us save these animals. Our helmets and life jackets gave us the appearance of predators emerging from the water, but the horse allowed us to approach and touch him. After assessing his condition, we haltered him. He showed absolute trust and allowed us to lead him into the water without hesitation.

The current was strong, and we were fighting hidden debris as we began to walk the horse upstream. The good news was our life jackets kept us from drowning; the bad news was their buoyancy prevented us from moving against the current easily. Isn't it ironic how the very thing protecting us was also threatening our safety?

More bad news—midway into the horse rescue effort, a news helicopter with apparently no better story to cover, flew over us and began to hover. This visibly upset the horse and put us at risk of being washed back downstream in the raging current. We motioned and motioned for the helicopter to fly away without success while the horse became more and more agitated.

I decided it was time to attempt to solve this problem or get fired from my volunteer position trying. It was clear the news helicopter was not going to leave, so with horse in one hand, I extended my free arm toward the helicopter, middle finger erect. I shot off the biggest birdie my middle finger could muster straight up to the whirly birdie. This seemed to work. I mean, they couldn't put that on TV, so they had nothing to air as long as I kept my finger up. If I got fired, so be it. At this point, a horse's life was at stake, not to mention my own. Volunteer job... or life? That's a no-brainer.

With both birds now gone, we calmed our brave horse down as quickly as possible and continued our upstream battle. We had been told there would be no additional release of water from the dam upriver. We had been lied to. In the middle of our rescue attempt, the water began rising-fast! In less than five minutes, the water rose from waist level to over our heads, and we were forced to swim alongside the horse who, at this point, was completely exhausted. We had to yell and yank hard on the halter to keep him from lying down and to keep him swimming. We had just a moment to make a major decision. Should we attempt to get him across a half-mile of rising current, or should we return him to the island and abandon him? If we tried to "save" him, he would likely drown. It we didn't, he would at least survive the night now.

This is how risk vs. benefit works: The risk to save the horse at this time, now that circumstances had changed, was too great because it put the rescuers' lives in jeopardy along with the horse's life. We had no choice but to turn back.

We made it back to the island with the horse. He was exhausted and trembling, and he could hardly stand. We doctored his cuts made by all the debris in the water, and with great sadness, we boarded the boat, hopeful another rescue could be attempted on him soon. We knew that he stood a greater chance of survival by sheltering in place than if we attempted to get him to land with the river rising. That didn't make it any easier to leave him there all alone. I prayed for him as we left him behind.

Rescue operations were cancelled from that location for two whole days because of the fear that homes would break away and wash downstream. During those 48 hours, I could think of nothing but that gentle horse. What the hell kind of rescue person am I? A prudent one. Yeah, sure. So what! You cannot imagine my joy to learn that the horse's owners found him by watching TV and were able to rescue him when the water receded on Wednesday. I learned from his owners that this horse had a remarkable survival instinct—he had swum 17 miles downstream from his flooded barn to the island where we found him! You won't believe this either. The owners told us that he still loves to swim in his pond! Sadly, his stable mates had drowned in the flood.

We rescued cats and dogs in different sections of town until dark. How surreal it was to be in a boat, in a landlocked state, in the center of town, riding across water over the tops of cars and road signs.

At dusk, we began another rescue. A woman had three cats trapped inside her home. We navigated to her home by boat on the basis of one identifying feature, the color of her home and the surrounding homes. Street signs and mailboxes were all submerged. As I slid off the boat and into the filthy water filled with sewage and every other contaminant known to man, I went underwater until my lifejacket brought me back to the surface.

The homeowner had fled, so the house was empty except for the cats. If riding on a boat down city streets had been surreal, this was even worse. I was chest deep in murky water, in the near darkness. The shades were all drawn and the power was off. Floating furniture and household items bumping into me below the surface gave the impression of an aquarium in need of a deep cleaning. I looked around as my eyes began to adjust, and I saw her three cats.

There were only three places in the living room above the water's surface, and a cat was perched atop each one of them. They were silent as their eyes fixated on me. It was heartbreaking to think they had been like this for days. I made my way over to the first cat, and she let me pick her up without clawing or even attempting to resist.

I carefully made my way to the door with her and then out to the boat. I had to be careful not to step off the porch, or I would be over my head in the water again. I passed her up to a rescuer in the boat who held her securely. We rescued the remaining cats and returned to the staging area where we handed off the cats to their owner.

She promptly placed two in her car, shut the door, and then dropped the third on the ground where it took off like a shot. Are you kidding me?!?! Was she out of her mind? "We risked our lives for your cats, and you just let one of them go," I implored!

I couldn't believe my ears when she told me he was the neighborhood stray and she didn't want him. We could have taken him to a shelter for heaven's sake. Everyone reacts differently under duress. I hoped this woman's senseless decision was attributable to the stress of the situation, and that under normal circumstances, she would have made a more humane choice.

There was no way to catch the traumatized cat at this point, and we were not happy campers! We scoured the neighborhood to see if we could find any other cats or dogs needing rescue from homes. When darkness came, we were forced to call off the mission for that evening. It was simply too dangerous. We had helped some animals and attempted to help others. Somehow it didn't feel like we had done enough, but we had done our best for a Monday. Beyond exhausted, we all returned home safely that night.

FINDING A NEW NORMAL IN THE LAND OF GRITS AND GREASE

Journal Entry – April 25, 2010
It's been what, two weeks since we set foot in Tennessee? Seems like a lifetime ago. I spend most of my time in the great abyss of grief and despair. I miss all that is familiar. I miss everyone I love in California. The pastor at church today hit four points really hard. Nothing I don't already know. Easy to hear when times are good, not so easy when times are bad. 1) God provides more completely in my weakness and pain (Damn that plan anyway!); 2) I need to receive His plan, not my plan for my life (But, why? Sometimes mine sounds so much better?); 3) I need to accept what I have as well as what I don't (Now there's the clincher—what if I can't? What if I just plain don't want to?); and 4) I need to find a new normal. (I've always considered normal to be far overrated and much too elusive. The only place I've been able to find it in my own life is the setting on my washing machine. If I couldn't find the old normal, how will I ever find the new one?) What I

want to say is, "That pastor's full of crap." What I know to say is, "He's right; it's all true."

I cry every day. Trapped between the reality of my new life and the fantasy of somehow believing I can have my "old one" back, I find my emotions strangely indescribable. They teeter between a numb place where I don't even remember if I like decaf or regular and a feeling place where I remember everything, and those memories seem to be centered in the middle of my chest pressing mercilessly until I can't breathe.

Don has returned to work. Angelina went back to school. Ryan found a job. I feel forsaken by the only people I know in this God-forsaken place. Like the patient in Room 202, Bed A, lying alone in the once-crowded hospital room after the Room 202, Bed B patient had been discharged, I feel more alone than ever. The boxes and piles of unpacked, unsorted, unorganized stuff mockingly stare at me as if to say, "Why did you bring us here? Send us back home where we belong." I can identify with their feeling of being out of place.

It seems like forever ago that we made the 2,000-mile, 40-hour journey in that terrible rainstorm. I can still hear the deafening thunder that accompanied that blinding lightening. How many times did we have to pull off the road to avoid getting struck? I think it was twice in Arkansas and once in Tennessee. Had God not promised never to flood the Earth again, I would have thought about a Home Depot run to buy wood suitable for an ark.

We've traveled so many miles in such a short period of time. Like the kid who gets to the amusement park and runs to the roller coaster everyone comes to the park to ride, only to find it's closed for repairs, I wonder what all the rush and excitement was about in the first place.

Journal Entry – April 27, 2010

I have no energy to write, but I must write. Writing keeps me sane (sort of). The storm kept me awake most of the night. It was all I could do to get my family (How can I say "family" when it's only half of it?) off to work and school. I need a nap. I want to sleep, but there is so much to do.

We are still without TV, phone, or computer thanks to the most recent storm. The repairman is supposed to come today. Does that mean I have to get dressed and let him in? I don't want to talk to anyone. I desperately want to talk to someone. OK, so good, someone's coming over, so I have to stay awake. I have to get dressed.

Under different circumstances, this big, bright, beautiful house could well be my dream house. It's twice as big as my house was in California, the house I never really liked but would give anything to have back. I aimlessly walk through the hallway, the many rooms. I feel trapped, isolated, lonely, and frightened. I keep feeling that I should go home now. "This is home," I remind myself. It hurts to say the word home. This place hasn't earned the title.

It just keeps raining, another tornado warning—no watch this time. What the hell is the difference anyway? That weather lady seems way too excited about the life- and property-threatening tornado. What is her problem? I don't even like her. I like the nice man on Channel 5 back home. There's that word again—home. Damn! The weather, my heart… will the sun ever shine again in either place?

Journal Entry – April 29, 2010

Tomorrow begins a new month. My first May in Tennessee. I long for comfort in my daily Bible reading. I feel I will drown in my tears if I do not get some relief. I implore the Lord to speak to my heart.

I read in passages from Isaiah 43 and 44: "When you pass through the waters, I will be with you; and when you pass through the rivers, they will not sweep over you. When you walk through the fire, you will not be burned; the flames will not set you ablaze. For I am the Lord, your God. I love you. Do not be afraid, for I am with you. I will pour water on the thirsty land, and streams on the dry ground. I will pour out my Spirit and bless you and your children."

I feel a little better, not because my circumstances have changed but because I remember God loves me, is sovereign, and is good. He will take me through these stormy waters. He will purify me in this fiery trial, but I will not be burned, just refined.

Journal Entry – April 30, 2010

I remember what I learned in my disaster relief chaplaincy training in California. People do generally recover from trauma and crisis. In time, they do get better. They can never return to the normal they once knew. They must find a new normal. That's it!!! I must find a new normal. I will recover, it will get better in time, it will be different, but it will be OK. I want to know how. I want to know when. I really want to know why. There are no answers today. There is the promise that the waters of despair and sadness will not sweep over me.

Looking back on these pre-flood journal entries post-flood, I can't help but wonder if there was something prophetic there. I don't know. What I do know is we came home that Sunday night, as the storm raged on, to find things in pretty good shape. Most of the stuff in the garage was drenched. We threw wet books and pictures into the trash, our wet clothes into the dryer, and our wet selves into the shower.

After allowing the warmth of the shower to take some of the chill off our bodies and minds, we braved a peek at the TV to see what we could find out about what was going on around us. The media coverage was alarming—it was hard to watch. Reporters said they weren't certain yet how much damage the flood had rendered. There were reports of people being trapped in their homes, of senior citizens having heart attacks. The words were disturbing. Only the visuals were more so: Cars floating, homes filled with water to eye level, people leaping into the water from their windows, rescue boats, frantic pet owners screaming, "Where's my dog? Please someone, do you see a little white dog with a red collar? Please find him."

The look of unbelief and confusion in people's eyes matched my feelings as I watched. As a psychotherapist, I well know that when nothing fits into any normal cognitive schema, the mind struggles to reject it. This made no sense, it was not part of my repertoire of human experience, and I tried to push it away as I have when I have seen such things on TV before. The problem was that it wasn't another country, or even another state where this craziness was happening. It was right here in my own backyard (literally)!

It's one thing to be an observer; it's quite another thing being a participant. Sure we could turn the TV off and try not to think about it, just close our eyes and go to sleep. Problem was, in the morning, it would still be there. It wasn't a faraway story happening to "those poor people in Nairobi," or even "those poor people in Louisiana." The story was up close and personal, very close and very personal. It wasn't going away with the push of a button on the remote.

It took a good while to fall asleep that night. Instant replays of the screaming people watching their belongings float away, the agonizing, desperate scream of the woman who couldn't find her dog played over and over in my mind. I kept wondering when and if Nashville would ever be "normal." (There's that word again.) And I kept wondering if we were safe. Would we have to evacuate our home again? Was the news report accurate? Was there something they weren't telling us?

The rain pounded the roof like a barrage of bullets firing from the sky. My chest was tight, my stomach upset, my head spinning. Sleep came—finally. Well, it must have, because I woke up to the next day.

WHAT? ANOTHER NEW NORMAL?

As the days went by, news of what was to become known as the Thousand-Year Flood began to disappear from the headlines and as it did, from my awareness and interest. It seemed to happen just as quickly as the sun-promoted return of the grassy fields from their temporary "lake" status. Media visuals of flooded property and debris left my TV screen and simultaneously my mind. My mind—the mind—searches for ways to return to normal, to restore to a previous level of functioning, attach to the known and familiar, "ground" us, and provide a sense of safety and well-being.

I had only been in Tennessee for three weeks, so for me there WAS no normal to return to. I wasn't functioning. Nothing was known or familiar. I was already dealing with my own traumatic event (the move and all the losses associated with it—children, extended family, friends, church family, income, foreclosure, job, sanity) before the flood. Quite frankly, the disappearance of flood-related news was, it shames me to say, a complete relief. I had so much on my mind already that I wasn't handling, how could I worry about this too?

Directly on the heels of our Tennessee flood, there were other national as well as international disasters. Nashville was lost in the clutter of more immediate, more important new coverage. Just before the flood, the BP oil spill in the Gulf had sucked the last breath out of the media. Then, of course, there was the more sensational news that crowded it out as well. You know the stuff I'm talking about—the stories that drive station ratings up—the fatal shooting, the corrupt politician, the drug bust in South America, and the high-speed chase. And so the flood, which I later learned was the costliest non-coastal natural disaster in U.S. history, was all but squeezed out by everything else going on. I took my cue from the media—I turned my attention to everything else going on in my own life. Don't get me wrong; there was still mention of the flood, but more like "yesterday's news" than a current event. It was kind of like a "side note," a ...P.S.

It wasn't really that hard to "forget" about it given that my immediate surroundings were void of the collateral damage seen on TV, and I wasn't getting out and about. Where? How? It appeared to be business as usual—school was in session, the sun was shining, neighbors returned to their morning jog, the church social was on the books. Reminders of the state being a national disaster area were not visible to me. Of course, I was managing my own collateral damage, my personal natural disaster, so I wasn't looking for reminders.

I find it interesting that when something doesn't directly affect us or doesn't directly affect us any longer, we tend to abandon our role as participant and return to the more comfortable, far safer role of observer. I had heard on the news that churches (of which there are four on every street corner in Nashville), and random citizens were banding together to help support the rebuilding of homes and lives. That's good. Someone is helping! The mayor had even named the restoration and recovery project "Nashville Rising." That's nice!

I have often wondered, looking back now, almost three years later, whether I would have done more in another place at another time. Had the places I saw on the news been familiar, would I have driven there? Had I been more together myself, would I have put on my Disaster Relief Chaplaincy shirt, hat, and badge and thrown myself into the mix as a Nashville Rising volunteer? I'd like to think I would have. It's what I normally do; only this wasn't normal, I wasn't normal. Yes! I can almost certainly say I would have had I been in California in familiar surroundings with familiar people, places, and people with meaning attached. You know what they say, "It's hard to take care of someone with the flu when you have a fever and are vomiting yourself!"

COMES THE DAWN

For the next 48 hours, we alternated between contemplating what lay ahead and taking care of immediate needs—banking, food, clothes, shoes, toiletries, and makeup. We were in dire need of makeup! For the first few days, bank withdrawals were limited to $200 per day, per person because the banks' computers were down, so our shopping excursions were limited. Through all the frenzy of rounding up basic necessities, we remained in the dark about the condition of our condos. The water had not fully receded, and while we were anxious to see the damage, we probably needed the extra time to prepare ourselves mentally and emotionally. We had a lot to process, but we would have much more to process when we finally gained entry to what used to be our homes.

In addition to the basics, I needed a car. By the time I realized we were going to flood, it was too late to get my car to higher ground, and it had flooded. Fortunately, I subscribe to the theory that "you've gotta have a person for everything." I have a superb mechanic who also happens to rebuild older, good-condition, one-owner, foreign cars. After repeated attempts, I finally got through to George.

"What have you got, George?"

"Nothing—I have no cars right now."

"What are you driving George?" For years, my family has bought cars that George drives—right out from under him. Every year, he buys a couple of cars, and he drives those cars while he rebuilds them.

"Well," he paused," I've got this little white BMW that I've completely rebuilt."

"I want it."

"Well," he paused again, "I've got someone who's interested in it."

"Well you just call them and tell them that someone has already bought it."

"Okay," he said.

"By the way, how much do want for it?"

"I want $6,000 total, including the rebuilt transmission and all the work I've put into it and will put into it before you get here. It's a 2000 BMW, and it's got some miles on it, but the way you drive, it'll last you 10 more years."

"Make that call," I said, thanking my lucky stars that I had scored a car. "I'll be there in a few days. Just hold it for me. You know I'm good for it, and I'll be there." Buying a car from George sight unseen was the least of my worries.

"I know. I'll see you when I see you. Take care," he said right before hanging up.

With that detail out of the way, I turned my attention to a few other mundane details, like buying a replacement cell phone in the hopes that a dry phone would provide reliable reception. It didn't—not for a week anyway.

Crack of dawn Tuesday morning saw a frenzy of activity as we prepared to survey the damage. We felt it would be devastating, but we hoped for the best. No amount of preparation could prepare us for what awaited.

On the drive to the condos, we wondered just how bad it could be. It would be awful; no, it would be okay. Back and forth we went, knowing that we were just filling dead air in the last few moments that our imagination would have to fill in the blanks.

My friends Lily and her sister-in-law Kerrie met me at the condo. I blew right past them and the damage on the first floor to learn the fate of my mother's kittens, Fifi and Fiona, tiny Abyssinian-mix rescues. There was no sign of them upstairs where I had abandoned them, and I went into a full-blown panic attack, struggling to breathe. A minute later, Fifi, the tiny, scrappy sister, popped her head out from under the bed. Fiona, the pleasingly plump sister, appeared right behind her. I would discover in the next few minutes that they were just about all that remained of my mother. Hadn't it been enough that I had lost her just a little over a year before the flood?

With that delightful reunion accomplished, I headed back downstairs, put on a pair of mud boots Lily had brought me, and began to survey what was left of the condo. The first floor—living room, dining room, kitchen, den, two bedrooms, two bathrooms, and an office—was a total loss. Six feet of water will do that. Only the upstairs bedroom and bath remained relatively intact. Unfortunately, I had left the window open after throwing Miss Fluff to the rescuers, so for the next eight hours, rain poured in.

I wasn't prepared for the sight that greeted me downstairs. Furniture had floated to other rooms, kitchen cabinets were wide open, and cooking vessels, plates, china, and utensils had floated from their proper place to anywhere and everywhere, including far corners of the condo. They mostly covered the kitchen floor, and the refrigerator had floated down onto the opposite counter. They don't make furniture like they did fifty years ago, but even the good furniture had crumbled like wet pieces of corrugated cardboard. Broken glass was strewn everywhere.

Some things were never recovered. Who knows where they floated once they made their way out the open office window. I have since heard stories of neighbors' belongings floating a mile or more down the Harpeth River.

I was immobilized by the sight of the devastation, having no idea what to do first. Lily and Kerrie jumped into high gear, relaying my instructions to everyone who was helping and overriding my instructions when they knew that emotion, not intellect, was speaking. That was most of the time. I didn't want to part with anything.

This was the second time Lily had come to my aid and led me around like a dog on a leash when I was completely overwhelmed. The first time was a little over a year before the flood, the day after my mother's second stroke in 48 hours—the day we learned she was going to die. Lily had taken another day off from work back then to shepherd me through the process of moving my mother from St. Thomas Hospital's pods (critical care units) to Alive Hospice, a few floors upstairs. Lily was obviously a true friend and a glutton for punishment.

My contractor Alfonso and his crew were waiting for us, and after giving me a big hug, he assured me that he'd find a way to put the condo back together in some fashion, no matter what I could afford. The future was another one of those "least of my worries." I just had to get through the present moment.

As the day progressed, little garbage piles began to form outside the condos, both in the front and in the back. My mind wandered back to the night before the flood when I looked into two of the closets packed to the brim with my mother's clothes. I remembered saying right out loud, "Mother, what will it take for me to let go?" A thousand-year flood was certainly not what I had in mind!

The night before the flood, I had also found a laminated card in her wallet sandwiched between old photos that read, "Miss me but let me go." I had looked at those photos 100 times since her death, and not once had I seen that card. Where did it come from? How could I have missed it?

Whatever—I had no choice but to let go of her things, and I didn't have time to dwell on her absence—not while I was ankle deep in God-only-knows what—floodwater, sludge, sewage, and toxins.

Moving the waterlogged furniture and personal belongings from the condos into those garbage piles was like digging through the remnants of our lives. Everything on the first floor joined my neighbors' belongings, which had bloomed into one gigantic garbage mountain out back by the pool. By the end of the day, what used to be our lives would be heaped 10 feet high in those piles. It was a sight unlike any I'd ever seen, and it was one I hope never to see again. Oh, but wait—I can dredge up those memories any time I like. Kerrie snapped her way through the day, documenting as much as her SIM card would hold.

ZERO DEGREES OF SEPARATION

Tuesday dawned, and we couldn't safely attempt any animal rescues due to the toxin level in the waters.

On Wednesday at 7:00 a.m., I received a call that Urban Search and Rescue (USAR) had been activated. I was a member of USAR, and my rescue dog and I were needed to assist in the flood recovery. I had been waiting for this call. I was also scheduled to begin work at a new job that very day. To ignore extending help to others went against everything in me. To miss the first day of a new job would likely make my first day my last. I chose deployment over employment.

We searched for most of the day in neighborhoods and trailer parks in what resembled a war zone in the Antioch area of Nashville. USAR remained on standby for other missions until Friday.

I did lose my job for not coming to work on Wednesday, but I would make the same decision again if faced with saving lives vs. a savings account. It's frustrating how shortsighted some can be. Here we were with Nashville under siege, and I was one of the few rescuers who had a dog certified to help with search and rescue. It wasn't a secret to anyone in town that Nashvillians were in a dire state of need. As fate would have it, I would never have gotten to work long-term flood recovery had I not taken this rescue assignment, so it was a blessing in disguise that I lost my job before I really had it.

That Friday night I got a call from a family friend requesting that we help look for a young man who was still listed as missing from the flood. He had gone tubing with two other friends on Monday. The water had torn their tubes apart and injured two of the friends, but the young man was still missing. I agreed to go out and help look for him.

Saturday morning, the two friends and others, including his girlfriend, met our search party at the point where he was last seen. My friend Anne once again joined me in the search. Another family friend who had search and rescue experience from his time in the military along with the missing man's friends joined us on-site. I prayed that we could find him but that his friends would not have to see him in that condition.

We searched most of the morning, and then thankfully, the Nashville Fire Department (NFD) and the new recruit class of the Nashville Police Department (NPD) appeared on the scene to aid in the search. We folded in with them as the new incident command and continued to work until dark. We were asked to return on Sunday to search again. When we returned Sunday morning, we found out his parents had driven in to help search for their son.

It was Mother's Day. Imagine the tragedy of looking for your missing son on that special day. Under normal circumstances, there would likely have been brunch, flowers, gifts, and cards. Instead, it was mud, debris, tears, and emptiness. We met his mother and then began to search for her son. There were no words to comfort her as she spent Mother's Day looking for his body among sewage, river waste, trash, and muddy, rushing floodwaters.

Our hearts were torn open, and the search took on a more personal meaning. The heroic members of the NFD, the very men and women who had been on boats from the start of the flood risking their lives, located his body days later and brought a teary, tragic closure to his family and friends. The rest of the flood recovery would be that way—personal.

Everyone had one degree or less of separation from knowing a survivor or a victim, including me. A childhood friend called and asked if I had any information on a friend of his. I had the unfortunate task of breaking the news to him that his friend was the first to go missing trying to get home to his children. His was one of the first bodies recovered. It was personal; it was in our own town, and we would know friends, family, and become friends with complete strangers through the course of working toward recovery. It was all so surreal. How could all of this be happening in a land-locked state, in the middle of town, our town? I had seen footage like this from Katrina and other disasters, but I had never imagined I would be rescuing dogs, cats, horses, and humans in my own town.

Forty-six counties out of the 66 counties with flood damage across the state would be declared federal disaster areas—that's about half of Tennessee. It would turn out to be the worst non-coastal water disaster in U.S. history. But it occurred during an attempted Times Square bombing and during the BP Gulf oil spill—and we rescued our own—so it wasn't 'newsworthy.'

The rallying cry became "We Are Nashville" as we were forgotten by the media and left to save ourselves. Save ourselves we did, and that saving continues to this day. You see, flood recovery continues well after the water recedes. After this disaster or any disaster of this magnitude is over, the on-going courageous work of recovery begins. I have worked in fire and rescue for over 21 years now, and this was the first time I had been a part of long-term recovery.

It was harder than any rescue mission I have ever worked. It has also taught me more about the human spirit and the importance of emotional support than I would have learned in 100 years of fire and rescue work alone. Here is where the real story of Tennessee's Thousand-Year Flood begins.

PART II

MJ – THE SURVIVOR

THE ROAD TO HELL... IS PAVED WITH GOOD INTENTIONS?

They say the road to hell is paved with good intentions. It would only be a few days before I would gain a firsthand, working knowledge of that saying.

Good news, what little of it there was, spread through the condos like wildfire in the days following the flood. A few days after the flood, I heard that a major relief organization was going door-to-door, handing out debit cards to help us with our immediate needs.

A few hours later, I was sitting in a patio chair under my carport to get some relief from the broiling sun when the volunteers arrived. Clutching my grandmother's black velvet bag against my chest, I was crying softly. Everything that belonged to my mother, father, and grandmother—my mother's watercolors, some of which I had recently matted and framed; my father's war photos of him as spy and an aviator; my grandmother's college diploma from Greece, her full-color wedding portrait, and a long ponytail of her blonde hair—was in the garbage heap a few feet behind the carport. That black velvet purse was all I had left of my grandmother, and I clung to it for dear life.

The volunteers asked me if I needed anything. I told them that I knew debit cards were available, and while I knew others were probably in greater need, I would be grateful if they could spare one.

The older woman looked at me and replied, "Honey, you don't need a debit card. You need a mental health worker."

"You have GOT to be kidding me," I said. "I have just been through a major trauma."

Then she disappeared... but not for long. A few minutes later, she and the 'mental health worker' appeared out of nowhere. The mental health worker said a quick hello and immediately pronounced a 'diagnosis' of post-traumatic stress disorder (PTSD), reciting a canned spiel on the subject. I let her finish, and then I let her know that I was well acquainted with the concept. Was I to understand correctly that without so much as a conversation with me, this woman was able to diagnose "my problem" as **post**-traumatic stress disorder when there was nothing "post" about the situation? I wasn't "post" anything; I was still in the thick of it!

I felt like I had been attacked without provocation, and I immediately became defensive. I felt the need to respond by recounting other times when circumstances had sent me and everyone around me into what she would term PTSD (which to me, the ordinary layperson, seemed a normal immediate response to each of these circumstances). I explained how my M.O. had always been to pull myself up and carry on with life after allowing myself to wallow for a few hours or days, depending on the circumstances. I had survived witnessing my mother's fatal stroke and the seeming ineptitude of the health care workers after the second stroke, including their refusal to call a doctor for several hours. (They handled the first stroke with immediacy, precision and professionalism in the emergency room, but Mother had been moved from the critical care pods to the floor when she had her second stroke, and that was an episode right out of *Keystone Cops*.)

I told the 'mental health worker' about dodging the first scuds in the Persian Gulf during Operation Desert Shield (even before war had been declared)—as a civilian—before the airline thought to supply the crews with protective gear, i.e., gas masks and suits. I went on to tell her about my co-workers and friends on flight 800 that fateful summer's evening when they were blown to smithereens above the Atlantic and about enduring the cover-up that followed. I told her that I could "teach the class on laughing at PTSD and getting on with your life" and that I had gotten along just fine through all of those experiences without the need of intervention from mental health workers.

Then she turned to me and prescribed the 'cure,' insisting that I should allow myself to cry and get it out. WHAT? I was having a *Twilight Zone* moment, one of many. That's exactly what I was doing—minding my own business, dealing with my grief on my own just fine until these people showed up and insinuated that I was crazy before they insinuated that I wasn't crazy. Did these people have day jobs as politicians?

I not only did not need her intervention, but more importantly, her proclamation that I should "allow myself to cry" infuriated me. That's exactly what I had been doing, but I didn't need her permission or blessing to work through my own feelings, and I didn't need validation of my feelings from any authority figure. I may have been furious, but this head-on collision with the nanny state served a purpose. It reminded me that no one can inflict their half-baked assessments on me without my expressed permission, nor can anyone validate my feelings without my consent. It doesn't matter what they think.

Before they moved on to their next prey, the "mental" woman (no, that's not a typo or a misprint) bestowed upon me some paper towels, bleach, and disposable gloves. I imagine she saved her debit cards for neighbors who were a little more mealy-mouthed and compliant—in other words, anyone but me.

From a survivor's perspective, this behavior was unacceptable. After that interaction, their organization will never receive one red dime from me. I learned long ago to contribute directly to individuals. I don't get a tax write-off, but I know where my contributions go. I know those who receive my contributions receive them with no strings attached and without judgment, and I know that instead of going toward ever-growing bureaucracies' "general funds," overhead, and bonuses, they will go solely toward those in need.

It was over a year after the flood before I learned that this organization had virtually "pulled people off the street," given them a few hours of training, and sent them into the field to care for our mental health. I was once again incensed, but at least during my encounter, I had enough sense to know that I didn't need to end up on some government list of uber-crazies, so I kept my real feelings to myself at the time.

The person who enlightened me in 2011 knew I was well grounded (literally and figuratively), so I went into a tirade about how much damage these workers could have done to people who were already emotionally drained by the flood—or worse, before the flood. I wondered how many people had been wrongly "diagnosed" and hoped there hadn't been any permanent damage done to some poor soul teetering on the edge somewhere. Or is this just some blanket diagnose applied to everyone who's ever been through a trauma?

My mother always said I was "bully" (an adjective, not a noun), meaning I could handle most anything without crumbling. In the face of this disaster, it took my last bit of strength to call upon my "inner bully" when dealing with "mental health worker" types. In retrospect, that encounter was instructive, and it strengthened me in the face of adversity.

Thankfully, most of my experiences with volunteers, government agencies, and private organizations were on a level far superior to what I experienced that day under the carport, and some of those individuals with whom I had encounters have turned into what I'm sure will be lifelong friends. In fact, the co-authors of this book, Melissa and Pam, are two of the individuals I had the privilege to meet during the aftermath of the flood and with whom I have been able to talk freely without fear of judgment or repercussion.

WELCOME TO THE FSA

Life after the flood was full of new and different adventures stretching my comfort zone to new dimensions. My next alien experience came the week after the flood when I asked for financial assistance. I had never been a card-carrying member of the Free Stuff Army (FSA), at least not until the flood, having always been on the other side of the donation chain. My parents had always encouraged me to give when I could and to do my best to make my way—I recall their words as if it were yesterday, "The world doesn't owe you a living."

To accept money was one of the most humbling and humiliating aspects of the flood for me; however, I got over it in short order. Without assistance, I couldn't rebuild, and I would have to move on and lose everything. If FEMA had allowed us to purchase flood insurance, we would not have been in need of their safety net. We were told that we were not located in a flood zone. (Oh really? You could have fooled me!) That is the reason they refused to underwrite flood insurance for us. River Plantation was once considered a flood zone—until it wasn't, sometime in the late '90s or early '00s. Talk about magical thinking.

In our section, every condo flooded. Only a couple of residents had flood insurance, and that was due to oversights by the mortgage holders (probably while their attention was diverted to scandalous robo-signing). Aside from those individuals, we were all in same boat, but everyone was thrilled for the people who were covered. Given that I had tried to get flood insurance and had been denied, I justified my induction into the FSA, regardless of how reluctant I was to join. I drew the line at the one-month offering of food stamps. The government was not required to feed me—flood or no flood. If others needed food, I'm glad there was help available, but I would feed myself, thank you. I'm stubborn that way.

I have always thought it should be easier for people to get jobs than to get assistance. But today, over 50 percent of all households receive government assistance, not including Social Security retirement benefits. So imagine waking up one day and finding yourself in a position where you felt you had to take help and add one more to those growing numbers!

From the burgers donated by Logan's to the free water from the water trucks no more than 10 minutes away at any given time, to FEMA and all the churches, organizations, and foundations, and to Garth Brooks, who performed many benefit concerts on our behalf, I was thankful. I had become a full-fledged, card-carrying member of the FSA, and I will never forget the generosity.

I lost my virginity (figuratively) with FEMA. I was not one of the first to ask for help because the thought of taking government or any other assistance appalled me. At the repeated insistence of a neighbor, I made the call—finally. I never would have placed that call except for her insistence and continual hounding. Thank God for my neighbor and her persistence.

Within a few days, the FEMA representative was at my doorstep, computer in hand, evaluating the damage to the condo. I had the required documentation because I had grabbed it at the last possible moment before the rescue and stuffed it into my purse. The FEMA representative could not have been nicer. It was anything but the humiliating experience I thought I would encounter. The mental health worker had left an impression and jaded my outlook toward soliciting or receiving help of any kind, but I would come to find that she was the exception rather than the rule.

In less than a week, FEMA transferred the maximum grant to my checking account. That was a heaven-sent gift. Now I could at least get the bones of the condo back in place. I knew it wouldn't begin to cover everything, but it was a nice start. I would worry about the rest later.

Just after I received the FEMA grant, we were dealt an unexpected blow. There was a possibility that some of the condos in River Plantation would be condemned. For the next few weeks, all we knew was that the possibility existed. Section X wasn't singled out for possible condemnation, but we had received the worst damage. It wasn't difficult to put two and two together. Rumors flew through the entire complex, but no one had the inside scoop.

Even then, I was in better shape than some of my neighbors were. Every scam artist in town had found their way to River Plantation. One neighbor was charged $25,000 just to gut the inside of the condo; others fared worse. Fly-by-night contractors had descended like vultures, and some residents had dished out money only to watch the vultures disappear before the work had even started. Again, you've "gotta have a person for everything," and I was thankful that I had an honest and reliable contractor. He adored my parents and went far beyond what he should have to ensure that their daughter would be able to come home.

During the limbo phase, I adopted a Scarlett mindset, not worrying about anything today that I could put off until tomorrow. Southern women seem to have a bit of Scarlett in them, so this was my Scarlett moment, my moment to conserve my strength and pace myself through dealing incrementally—frankly, dealing with as little as possible at any moment. There would be plenty of time to deal with things later. This survival technique—dealing with things in bite-size chunks—would get me through the aftermath of the flood. It's not ideal, of course, but there's something to be said for procrastination in the face of overwhelming circumstances. When you're in the thick of it, you do whatever you have to do just to get through it.

I've always wanted to see the conclusion at the beginning of a project, but I would have been immobilized if not for my Scarlett attitude. Not only that, but after I released my raging fury toward God, "You caused this; now you can jolly-well take care of it because I don't have a clue where to begin," I calmed down. From that point forward, my worry level diminished. It didn't go away, but it was manageable. I stopped alternating between hyperventilating and heart palpitations every time I thought about my future.

As the weeks and months wore on, things did begin to fall into place. FEMA was a huge surprise, and there were many others in store along the path to recovery. All the while, during the good and the bad, I couldn't help but think, "Do I deserve any of this?"

One miserable day in July when the thermometer tipped well over 100 degrees in the shade, I had to spend hours on end at the condo. With no air conditioning and just a little air circulating from the fans, I can only guess that temperatures rose above 120 degrees inside the condo. I began to feel faint and sick to my stomach, and the next day I knew it was severe heat exhaustion. I had heat exhaustion as a child, and you never forget the feeling.

As I lay in bed, the phone rang, and caller ID showed my priest's number. Oh NO! I was too sick to make up some excuse about rarely darkening the church door. I wasn't going to admit that after attending my mother and father's funerals in such rapid succession it would be a cold day before I came back to church. I toyed with not answering the phone, but in the end, I decided to face the music. To my utter astonishment, I learned the archdiocese had taken up a collection for flood survivors, and the priest was getting ready to distribute the monies! They say a mother's job is never done, and I believe that Mother jumped into action up there in heaven, serving as my advocate.

This was just the beginning of the blessings that flowed my way. I couldn't have imagined the obscure corners from which help would arrive—and always just in the nick of time. The tide was turning.

THE LONG AND WINDING ROAD HOME

The summer of 2010 gave new meaning to the word "layover." When we flew the troops during the Gulf War, we joked that our hotel was the "Hotel California." We checked out on occasion to fly back to the states, but we didn't **leave** Rome for over a year. The flood necessitated another extended layover away from home. Unlike the days of Operations Desert Shield and Desert Storm, 200 of my closest friends weren't at my side during the flood aftermath, but the friends and neighbors surrounding me were worth their weight in gold.

After regaining transportation, my next move was to the Microtel, which was inhabited mostly by flood survivors and many of my neighbors. We met downstairs each morning for breakfast, and if you didn't know better, you would have thought we were a group of friends on vacation enjoying a few days in Nashville. The hotel staff extended special courtesies and relaxed the rules to make us feel at home. The front desk served as a communications center, passing on information about meetings, get-togethers, and recovery services.

My surviving cats were welcome there, and they settled right into life in the hotel. They're extremely adaptable. I wonder how much easier our lives would be if we took a lesson on adaptability from the animal kingdom.

After three weeks at the Microtel, I resumed the long journey home with many stops along the way. Next, I moved to my friend Malvina's house in Franklin, and my cats settled in just down the road at her daughter Lily's house. Lily's family, especially her son Dylan, cared for the cats, though I would check in on them almost every day. Malvina didn't have Internet connectivity, so I briefly moved back to the Microtel sans cats before moving to Lily's, where I would spend most of the rest of my time until moving back into the condo. But home is not a physical structure; it's a place where we feel safe and cared for. For now, home was Lily's, not a shell of a condo.

I had known Lily since we were kids, and over the past eight years, we have also been colleagues, but I did not know her husband or her two children well. That would all change as Ray, Dylan, and Megan welcomed me into their family. Even their pets became like my own; I have since adopted Georgie, their huge yellow tabby due to circumstances that prevent them from keeping him. He is a constant reminder of their kindness to me and the wonderful time I spent under their roof. At the end of each day, when we were all together, cooking and eating dinner, it was like there was no flood. It was like spending an extended vacation with friends and family—until the next morning when I would return to Bellevue.

By mid-July, the daily trek from Franklin to Bellevue was wearing thin—60 miles round trip. Because my life had been a series of crises over the previous 18 months (my father also had died just a few months before the flood), there had been little time to digest any of them. After life settled down at Lily's, the past started to crash in on me—hard.

The incident that sent me over the edge happened one afternoon at Starbucks. I was working on my computer when I received a disturbing email. With that, the coffee cup flew out of my hand and landed squarely on my computer. As a former geek, I knew the most prudent choice was to shut down the computer hoping to save it. Or, I could finish an assignment as quickly as possible and email it to a client, knowing it would destroy the computer. I chose to finish the assignment as quickly as possible and email it to the client, knowing in advance the consequences. I had to make the deadline and forfeit the computer. My last $2,000 later, I was set up with a new computer and an updated bundle of software necessary to do my job. The original software discs had floated down the Harpeth River.

With this first of many "last straws," I found myself needing to leave Lily's house just to get in a good cry. I didn't want to break down at the house because I didn't want anyone to think I was ungrateful for all they had done to help me. The crying jags were now coming daily, and I was running out of places to run and hide. It was time to get out of there.

I tried to get back into the Microtel, but there was no room at the inn. A neighbor of mine managed to get me into a long-term, residence-type hotel, a last stop for those on their way to homelessness. It was not far from the condo, and I was lucky to find a room. To Bellevue residents, it's known as "the Meth Lab." In 2005, an explosion initially reported as originating from a homemade meth lab in one of the rooms proved false, but the legend and the name have stuck. I remember checking in. The clerk asked me if I'd like to see the room. I didn't; I just wanted a room—any room would do. How bad could it be?

After hauling my bags up three flights of stairs and around to the back, I flopped on the bed, and the dirty pink wall color began to sink in. Roaches appeared occasionally only to scurry back to their hiding places once they spotted me. These roaches were no match for their New York cousins, but they were still roaches. You could actually see through what passed for towels, and I haven't found the proper descriptive word for the faint odor that clung to every piece of fabric in the room. Clearly, my next step was to buy some cleaning supplies and get to work.

I called my friend Kathy to vent. She and I have been the sisters we never had since our first year in high school at St. Cecilia. I LOST IT on the phone with her. I felt no need to fill her in on the other dreary details, just the pink walls. "Pink walls," I said, as I launched into a tirade about those pink walls. "Dear God, it's a good thing Fifi [my mother] isn't here to see this." I was freaking out. It's a good thing that mental health worker was nowhere to be found, or I surely would have been institutionalized.

Kathy was in no mood for this. She had not been well, and I caught her at a very low moment. I skipped over the other details of my new home, concentrating only on the pink walls.

Kathy gave me a good, swift kick in the butt and told me, "Just get over it," just like Fifi would have done.

That was all the push I needed. Somehow, I did just get over it. My mother and the airline had trained me well—to just get over things. Somehow, I drew upon that skill: Live in the present and appreciate the moment for whatever its worth. Home is where you are NOW! I had learned from the day of the flood to trust others who could be trusted, and I had learned another new skill—to listen to others when it mattered.

Within a few days, I had settled into a new routine, and the Meth Lab became my temporary home. It even started feeling like home—my, how my standards had deteriorated! I learned that it is possible to cook real food with nothing more than a stovetop and one All-Clad pan. Years later, the irony of sautéing dinner in the Meth Lab instead of grabbing a Big Mac like a normal person strikes me as funny.

Drawing on my years of living in The Big Apple, I fell back into taking precautions such as never going out past dark (though I went out past dark all the time in New York) and developing a hyperawareness of my surroundings. I answered the phone the first time it rang, but that was the last time I made that mistake. I kept reminding myself that I would get beyond this and laugh about it someday. In fact, I got to the point where I could laugh while I was still there. I knew it was temporary and it, too, would pass. I found humor in whatever dark corners it lurked.

One night when friends picked me up for dinner, I told them to meet me in the lounge for happy hour. There was no lounge; there was no happy hour; there was no lobby. There was only a reception cubicle behind some kind of glass or Plexiglas wall—bulletproof if they were smart. We all had a good laugh when they realized I was pulling their legs.

Two years later, I would give Kathy complete details, and her reply was simply, "DEAR GOD, I had no idea! I told you to stay at my condo."

At the end of August, I moved back to Malvina's to care for her dog while she went to Greece. In the meantime, I had collected more "essential stuff." My life became a George Carlin routine in reverse. Instead of shedding stuff, I was collecting it. Considering I had started out with the clothes on my back, I was now laden down with riches.

Hauling even more bags down those three flights of stairs, I thought I was going to pass out. It was another grotesque dog day of summer, 100+ degrees in the shade. The desk clerk took one look at me when I checked out halfway through packing my car, and she graciously jumped into action, helping me move the rest of my stuff down those three flights of rickety stairs. Imagine the additional publicity of a flood survivor dropping dead during checkout! Why, oh why, did this summer have to be one of those off-the-chart hot summers?

After a couple of uneventful weeks at Malvina's, I hauled everything back to Lily's, where I spent the rest of my sabbatical.

During my time on the road, the women who met for coffee every Wednesday back at the Section X clubhouse moved the weekly gathering to City Limits, our neighborhood coffeehouse. We came from near and far for this ritual. It was thanks to City Limits' owner that our group first met Melissa, who at that time, worked for Tennessee Recovery Project.

Melissa and one or more of her co-workers were guests at our weekly coffee klatches for most of the summer. They listened patiently while we vented, and they laughed at all the appropriate moments. They were quick with resources when anyone needed a helping hand, but most of all, they listened. At first, we were reserved and cordial, but that didn't last long. By the third week, they saw us in our raw form—the way we always were.

At 20 to 50 years our junior, I suspect they didn't realize middle age (and older) women could "let loose." If we laughed, whined, and vented before, we managed to take it to greater heights in the aftermath of the flood. It was our way of coping, of letting it out once a week with others who had gone through the same event, and while our guests were welcome, we were not about to change our M.O. for anyone. Love us or leave us. They loved us and stayed.

HOME AT LAST

Moving day had finally arrived more than six months after the flood. I would have a home once again—and not one day too soon. I was elated to get home.

I had spent the first couple of weeks of November cleaning construction dust a few hours a day, only to find the next day that it had multiplied overnight. The more I cleaned, the more it reappeared. I spent several nights upstairs when I was too exhausted to drive back to Lily's after a day of doing battle with the dust. It was creepy up there—no security system, no landline, no cable, spotty Internet service borrowed from my next-door neighbor, and two channels on the five-inch digital TV. The eerie sound of silence hung heavy like an early-morning autumn fog over the retaining pond out front.

Nothing mattered more than being home and returning my cats to their home. I wondered if they would realize that this was "home" after spending so many months of their short lives away from home. What would they think when they first saw "their room"? Would they recognize it? What would be going through their minds? I have always wished dogs and cats could speak—but never more than at that moment.

It didn't matter that I still didn't have backsplashes in the kitchen, a working fireplace, rugs on the floor, furniture and a TV in the den, or a kitchen table. Nothing mattered except that I was home. The rest would take care of itself, and somehow it did, but certainly not on my timetable.

When I first moved home, the downstairs had six sticks of furniture—a new bed and chest of drawers along with a chest given to me by neighbors in the master bedroom and a sofa, love seat, and glass-top coffee table—the only piece of furniture that survived the flood—for the den. The new sofa and love seat were still in the living room, out of the way while the contractors worked in the den, and they were too large to shove through the interior doors. I would have to wait for the contractors to move them out the front door, around the side of the building and in through the back door when they finished working in the den. In the meantime, I moved one of the chairs from the patio into the kitchen where I would sit at night and gaze in wonder at the progress that had been made.

The night I moved home, I received a kitten born the day of the flood and rescued the next day. It was a Norwegian forest cat, just like Miss Fluff—talk about the circle of life. This kitten was a lifesaver when it came to getting through the next 18 months. I immediately fell in love with Zorba the Cat, and he was a constant reminder of my many blessings since the flood—and he reminded me how lucky we both were to be alive.

The day after I returned home, I received another one of those "just-in-time" miracles. Melissa showed up at my door with an array of kitty toys, a kitty condo, and a Nashville Pet Products gift certificate. Now I didn't have to worry about feeding my cats, and they would have toys to occupy them while I attempted to put my life back together.

I soon discovered that my heat didn't work. Since I was able to afford reconstructing only the bare bones up to this point, I certainly didn't have the money to fix the heat. I dressed in layers, and stayed warm at night by piling on every comforter and blanket I could find in the attic. I would have to pick up a few extra writing jobs to afford heat. That was easier said than done, so after a few weeks of sub-freezing nightly temperatures and warming water on the stovetop by day, I scraped together enough money to fix the furnace.

A week before Thanksgiving in 2010, the friends who gave me Zorba called and said that they thought it would be nice to have a "Plaster Thanksgiving." (You have GOT to be kidding me!) Some last-minute miracle from somewhere would have to land on my doorstep for me to pull this off.

"Sure," I said, trying my best to sound sincere. "Come on over for Thanksgiving dinner." I didn't have two nickels to rub together, I had no idea how I would buy food, and we would have to sit around the coffee table in the den to eat, but somehow, I would pull it off.

The day I moved home, I had learned from someone in a checkout line that an organization was providing flood survivors with $500 gift cards. I had applied, and I had completely forgotten about it until after I agreed to host the dinner. I would soon receive a gift card for Trader Joe's, but would it arrive in time for Thanksgiving?

As the week wore on, I became exceedingly anxious, but it arrived two days before Thanksgiving. I took full advantage of TJ's ready-made Thanksgiving sides (something I would never do under normal circumstances), and they were not only edible, they were delicious under the circumstances—a gift from heaven. With only two days to go and a limited supply of small appliances, kitchen gadgets, herbs, spices, and condiments, this was no time to exercise culinary creativity. I brined and grilled a turkey and bought a "tofurkey" for the vegetarian.

A few days before Thanksgiving, the contractors moved the den furniture back to the den. The friends with whom I shared Thanksgiving had given me a beautiful leather chair and matching ottoman that was available as the result of another couple's divorce. The backsplashes were in place in the kitchen, and the see-through fireplace was in. The unpainted mantel and fireplace surround in the den had been installed, and the place continued to come together. Thanks to the kindness of strangers and friends alike, Thanksgiving dinner was a resounding success.

I had never, *ever* served guests prepared food. I couldn't help but wonder if lowering my standards without freaking out meant I was in some kind of downward spiral, but in the end, I gave myself credit for handling something beyond my control with grace—grace under pressure.

SETTLING IN

After the flood, I had been forced to drop a number of clients. I could now turn my attention to finding work. It took four solid months to add to my pared-back client list. At one point, I seriously questioned my ability to write. I thought I had lost the touch.

It had been a while since I had added new clients because caring for elderly parents takes much of your time and energy. I had spent the 13 months before my father's death caring for him during his decline. Even while he was in assisted living, I made daily trips to the facility and brought him meals cooked from scratch. Would you want to eat institutional food? I wouldn't, given the choice.

The process of querying had changed, but I hadn't received the memo. It had been cut back from submitting proper page-long queries to submitting a couple of paragraphs with links and maybe a resume. What's next? Text messages? YouTube replies?

One day I was debating with a colleague whether YouTube or the lack of attention span had come first, and the lightbulb went off. I applied the hypothesis to querying. Each query I have submitted since that debate has been two to three short paragraphs with my resume and a list of links at the bottom. Soon, writing assignments were flowing like black crude during the oil rush (or at least enough for me to keep the cats fed).

In March 2011, I finally received approval from We Are Home, a local organization funded by the Garth Brooks benefit concerts through the Community Foundation, for a grant. It had taken nine months to get this grant, and each time they said "no," I spoke even louder, saying "YES!" I think they grew tired of my calls and figured out I wasn't going away. By the time I dealt with We Are Home, I had become a renegade flood survivor. I was scripting my future rather than letting my circumstances script it.

I took a lesson from the salesperson playbook. "No doesn't mean 'no'; it's a cry for more information." I am not cut out for sales, but when you're desperate, you'll try anything. In this case, my dogged persistence paid off.

That grant allowed me to pay off more of the bare-bones construction that had been completed since their inspector had visited in September 2010.

One day during the spring of 2011, Melissa stopped by again. She had just moved to an organization called the United Methodist Church Committee on Relief (UMCOR). This organization was active in Tennessee meeting unfulfilled basic needs of flood survivors. I sure had plenty of those, but I wasn't hopeful that they would help me because I had received so much help already. I was wrong, and I couldn't believe my luck.

From that point through July 2011, I had a bevy of volunteers from all over the country working on my condo. During the summer months, various youth groups traveled to Tennessee, and they were "my kind of teenagers," a throwback to my era of growing up, something that we see little of these days. They were respectful (in front of adults), eager to learn new skills, loved the cats, and they were fun to have around. They reminded me of me when I was a teenager—fun loving with a knack for dancing right up to the line without crossing it—at least not where the adults could see the antics. These kids were a treasure. Their team leaders and chaperones were as much fun as the kids were, and they were all delightful to work with.

While I was painting the new fence with my all-time favorite crew from Texas, one of the team leaders spotted something unusual. There is a partial knot in the wood in each of two planks where they meet, and the two knots form a heart. I remember the tears welling in our eyes when we noticed it. It was one of those things you just know is a sign, and it was a sign of the loving work they were putting into my condo. They were part of the healing process.

By the time they headed back to Texas, the condo was much closer to being finished. They built a new fence for the patio because the old one had buckled under the pressure of the water. It was a wonder it hadn't collapsed. They insulated the shed that backs up to the master bath. By the time they left, the master bathroom was borderline functional, the guest bathroom had running water, two optional doors had been installed to corral the cats, the kitchen cabinets finally had pulls, among other things.

After the crew left, I received a beautiful black-and-white framed photograph, signed by each of the kids and their leaders. It will hold a special place in my office when I get around to decorating it, and it will always hold a special place in my heart.

At some point during the summer of 2011, Melissa introduced me to Pam. We are not just co-authors thrown together to write a book. We are three friends who experienced the flood separately but whose lives intersected during the aftermath of the flood—right place, right time, right chemistry, and this book is the result of our friendship as well as our separate and shared experiences of the Thousand-Year Flood.

Christmas 2011, my friends Carole and Terry came to Nashville for a visit. I worked night and day to pick up work to add a few more touches. Friends had already donated many things for the den—lamps, a beautiful cabinet, and ornate matching Grecian pots, one of which functions as the base for a side table in the den.

Thanks to my work frenzy, I was able to buy the area rug for the den that I had coveted since the week after the flood. I finally got a chandelier for the dining room, pulls and shower curtains for the downstairs bathrooms, and lighting and towel racks for the master bathroom. I had a brand new down comforter, lamps, and bedside tables for the master bedroom where Carole and Terry would stay.

I had already bought a beautiful wrought iron and glass fireplace protector for the den side of the see-through fireplace, and I bought another one for the dining room side to keep the cats out of the fireplace. It had been the focus of their curiosity from day one, and I had visions of them exploring a live fire. The office was still a junk room, so I closed the doors and kept it out of sight. The place wasn't anywhere near finished, but it was presentable and comfortable.

Lily and her family moved to a smaller farmhouse the weekend after Thanksgiving, so I was storing her huge kitchen table in the dining room and a bed in the guest bedroom. UMCOR secured a chest of drawers, mirror, and bedside stand for that bedroom as well. Kathy gave me a sofa, table and lamp, two chairs, and coffee table for the living room and a kitchen table and chairs. I was good to go for company. My friends and I had a wonderful visit over Christmas. We put up a tree, and we decorated the den. Most of my Christmas decorations had drowned, but I found two bins of Christmas decorations in the attic. I had overlooked them when I moved the rest of the Christmas decorations to a spare closet downstairs. I couldn't believe my luck because we had just enough ornaments to cover the tree.

I finally bought "guest" dishes and flatware to replace the china and silver that floated down the Harpeth River, and I hosted 10 for dinner on Christmas Eve. Things were beginning to return to normal, and what better time to be able to say that than during the Christmas holidays!

Before the holidays, Melissa asked if I had lost anything of sentimental value during the flood, "like a medal." Yes, I had! My Desert Storm civilian medal had vanished during the flood like so many other things.

Melissa dropped by while Carole and Terry were here and brought a Christmas present. She insisted that I open it then and there. It was the civilian Desert Storm medal, framed in a black shadow box. Carole and I both started crying. We had each been presented with the medal in a ceremony in New York the year after the Gulf War ended, and it brought back so many bittersweet memories, especially memories of our friends who had died on flight 800. That gift was the exclamation point on a perfect Christmas.

Carole came without her husband for a weeklong visit in September 2012. I learned well in advance of her trip that she was coming, so I jumped into action once again during the summer. This time, I bought two new rockers to replace the dilapidated gliders on the patio, and I replaced the faded tan umbrella canopy with a bright-red one. I planted just enough flowers to make the patio inviting. I even grew melons and vegetables on the patio, and we enjoyed the fruits of that labor at the dinner table. The junk room was no more; it was an office. Kathy had furnished the office with a desk, sofa, lamp, and cabinet.

The week before Carole came, I replaced the missing built-in bookcase in the den, and that one item made a huge difference. As I looked around the den, I realized that I could not have planned a more appealing den if I had picked out all the pieces myself. I put the final touches on the guest bathroom, and finally, I replaced the broken window and the windows with broken seals. The trim work is almost finished, and I believe that within the next six months to a year, my punch list will be complete.

My walls are still void of art, and I do not have permanent blinds on the windows. I have finally learned patience, and each new addition I get to make is like ripping open the gift wrap on Christmas morning as a child. It may take years to fully furnish and decorate my condo, but if I never were to add another stick of furniture, I would still be content just knowing that I am home.

Disasters have a way of changing your perspective. After you get beyond your initial impatience, you learn that the plan will come together as it is meant to unfold and not on your timetable.

THE PAUSE THAT REFRESHES? NOT!

What is it about weather events in Middle Tennessee and the second of the month? Friday, March 2, 2011, was another tense day across the South. Unless you live in a tornado alley, you can't possibly know the fear that grips you when you know tornadoes are headed your way. There's nothing quite like an eminent tornado to shove the flood you survived right out of your mind.

Unlike those surprise-attack tornadoes, we had plenty of time to prepare for this one. If you take a direct hit, you're probably history no matter what you do, but for the first time, it occurred to me that if the hit were indirect, comprehensive preparations could matter. For some reason, the thought "lock down this place like you're preparing an aircraft for an emergency" entered my mind—"emergency," of course, being a euphemism for "crash."

Perhaps my reaction was because this was the first time I remember a feeling of total terror engulfing me before a weather event. Maybe you view disasters differently after you've personally survived one and "it happens to other people" no longer applies. Or perhaps it was my mind telling me to stay busy so I wouldn't dwell on the possible outcome. Whatever it was, I sprang into action.

When I say locked down, I mean LOCKED DOWN! I cleared all counters and lateral surfaces on the first floor and cleared away most of the second floor. Most of my neighbors and I had long since moved irreplaceable possessions and documents to the second floor—just in case we should flood again. But this wasn't going to be a flood. If anything, the roof was more likely to blow off first. So NOW I had to haul everything important back downstairs and lock it away.

I had cleaned out my storm closet after the surprise, middle-of-the-night tornadoes in January. But this gnawing feeling about flying missiles had been drilled into my head decades before at TWA, and I couldn't shake it. Next, I cleared the patio of everything except the patio table and chairs. I locked the grates and the burner covers from the gas oven in the dishwasher. (Talk about paranoid!) I locked all the interior doors in case the windows were blown out. I wanted to put something between the flying glass and the interior "safe area." The few remaining family photographs, important documents, computer, and Passport drive went into the storm closet. This place was locked down like Fort Knox.

I already had a set of tornado litter boxes and extra food and water in the guest bathroom, which was just outside the storm closet, for the cats. It's on a windowless, exterior brick wall, but the pipes provide extra protection. My tiny digital TV, which can pick up a couple of local stations, went into the closet. The walk-around weather radio was clipped to my jeans. The walk-around phone was in my pocket, and the cell phone was in the storm closet—along with comforters, pillows and blankets, and my "weather purse"—a purse the size of a tote bag that I had packed to the brim and flung from the second story down to the rescue canoe during the flood.

Thanks to my neighbor, I stocked the closet with water and snacks. She had heard stories of people who were missing for days but had survived because of water and a few snacks, something that hadn't occurred to me. Good idea. I was ready. Bring it on.

Now, with everything locked down, there was only one thing left to do—work myself into a frenzy watching Nancy Van Camp and crew from WSMV as they delivered minute-by-minute gory details and tracked the progression of the tornadoes. Some meteorologists thrive on "weather events," and Nancy especially seems to love her job when disaster hangs heavy in the air. By the time the storm reached Dickson, 15 miles from here, Nancy had whipped me into a full-on panic, and I was just about ready to jump out of my skin. Where were those mental health workers now?

My overwhelming concern was my cats. What if I didn't make it and they did? Who would care for them? Thankfully, during the last drill, they had all followed me into the storm closet right before I closed the door. This time would be different. The novelty of the storm closet had worn off. I spent the five minutes before barricading myself in the closet chasing down the cats, but the only one I could corral was Fifi, the tiny one. I snatched her and headed into the closet. I knew in the back of my mind that Melissa would tend to finding them good homes if anything happened to me, and that helped a little.

Just as I shut the door, Melissa called to give me updates on the progress of the tornadoes. I asked her to call back when they got to our immediate area.

When she called back, the last thing I expected to hear her say was, "I don't want you to freak out, but the tornado is heading down Sawyer Brown Road" (the main road running the length of River Plantation).

"SAWYER BROWN ROAD? You have GOT to be kidding me! Right through River Plantation? Please take care of my pets if anything happens to me," I begged her. How could any neighborhood be so unlucky? After we hung up, I heard a cacophony coming from the front yard.

Melissa was back on the phone giving me updates on wind speed—100, 102, 105 mph! I told her that it sounded like things were thrashing around outside.

When I mentioned that the howling was intermittent, she said, "That's not a tornado hit. The noise would be sustained if the tornado touched down."

I remember asking her if I was going to die today—using similar words I had used during the flood and during the scud incident during Gulf I. Three times before, I had cheated death. They say that you relive your life right before you die. I didn't relive my life, but in the space of a few seconds, my mind raced through each of those other close calls: the flood, inbound scuds in the Persian Gulf, and the time I caught (or rather, didn't catch) a wave in Puerto Vallarta. Not only did I almost drown, but I was also thrown up on the beach, startling an older couple when I landed at their feet, gagging and spewing water all over them. I relived those moments simultaneously, like a patchwork quilt of terror. I'm not sure how that's possible, but it happened. I started crying and asked Melissa to babysit me on the phone until the tornados had passed.

She reassured me that she would have a rescue (and "recovery," though she had the good graces not to say that word) crew headed to River Plantation post haste if the tornado touched down.

I remember saying, "Well, I might not BE here, but if I am, I'll join you in the rescue."

In the moments after we hung up, I wondered if I should pack up and leave Nashville. Some tornado seasons are worse than others, but we do live in a tornado alley, and that's not going to change. While we probably won't die from a New Madrid event, we will be affected. Hadn't I had enough of natural events?

As I weighed the pros and cons, it occurred to me that in addition to Nashville being a beautiful city and one of the most livable cities in the U.S., the entire population, from the mayor on down, had pulled together and brought us through the flood. I remembered thinking how lucky I was not to live in New Orleans during Katrina, and it dawned on me that no matter what the disaster, Nashville would react like Nashville and care for her people. I was a Nashvillian, and nothing would deprive me of my birthright. As long as I live in this country, I will probably live here. As I pondered this, the full meaning of "We Are Nashville" sank in.

Now that I've lived through a flood **and** a tornado passing directly overhead, I have learned a lot. It occurs to me that when you live in a tornado alley and a flood zone, you have to be adaptable and ready to spring into action, and you must be nimble enough to change course at a moment's notice.

A weather radio is a necessity, not a luxury. I have two, but the one I rely on most is the radio version of a walk-around phone. The other one is a battery/solar/hand-crank AM/FM/ weather/shortwave radio for use in a worst-case scenario—an extended period without electricity.

The object in preparing for a tornado is to minimize damage, assuming a lack of total devastation. Flying missiles are the greatest concern in a tornado if the windows break, allowing high winds to blow through the structure.

First, make a checklist. It's a work in progress until you've been through a few weather events. Aviation Analyst and former commercial pilot John Nance has recommended the checklist idea to hospitals to help remove human-driven errors. If the idea is good enough for aviation and health care, we mere mortals can adapt it to our needs.

After retiring from TWA, my friend Carole worked at a hospital in the operating room. The OR adopted this procedure a few years ago, and she says it has made a huge difference. Procedures are now handled with clocklike precision, and every routine pre-op and post-op is identical thanks to the checklist.

Keep your car full of gas so you don't have to compete for a place in line right before a weather event. Stock your pantry with enough non-perishable foods to last at least a week, but preferably a month, to avoid a last-minute rush to the grocery store when you have to fight with everyone else for limited groceries on the shelf. Keep an emergency supply of cash on hand, in case the computers go down at your bank. We have to be responsible for ourselves. If electricity goes down all over town, it may take weeks to restore power to all areas of town as it did after Nashville's ice storm in 1994.

Keep all vital records, papers, and mementos together in a zippered freezer bag inside a plastic bin or portfolio, moving them upstairs/downstairs depending on the weather event (flood vs. tornado). Better yet, scan everything possible, put it onto a thumb drive, and keep another copy offsite. Be careful about uploading to those cloud services. If you read the fine print, they (not you) sometimes own the material. Once you upload your information, you lose control of it.

Keep designated areas free for stashing glass, knives, lamps, etc.—anything with the potential of turning into a flying object—and put them away before a tornado, time permitting. Clean out your safe area ahead of time, and store items you'll need in that area. Don't forget the water and snacks, and remember to make provisions for your pets. Pray to your selected deity, the universe, whatever, and if possible, remain on the telephone with someone during the worst part of the event. That way, you have support, and you have a lifeline to real-time information. Keeping a communication line open also provides you with someone who knows if something goes terribly wrong, and that someone will ensure that help gets to you.

We have chosen to live in this beautiful city, but it comes with a price—weather events. You have to take the good with the bad. Lucky for us, the good far outweighs the bad. The better prepared we are, the more likely we are to come through the event with the least amount of damage and the better position we'll be in to help those who may not be so fortunate.

PAY IT FORWARD

We've all heard the expression "pay it forward," but what does it mean to a disaster survivor? While we accomplish many things in life on our own, I didn't see one disaster survivor who made it to the other side without help from others. Those "others" paid it forward in their service to the survivors.

Paying it forward doesn't mean performing random acts of kindness with the expectation of receiving something in return. It means performing those acts because you want to, because performing those acts IS the payment and the gratification. Watching someone's eyes light up in delight is all the individual who pays it forward needs in return. It also doesn't mean writing a check to your church or an organization and calling it a day.

Think back to the people who have gone the extra mile for you when they had nothing to gain. Those are the people who have paid it forward. After the flood, an entire army of people paid it forward to help me out. I never wanted for a roof over my head, food to eat, empathy and guidance, not to mention the material things that friends and strangers donated to make my life much easier. All of those people have paid it forward in spades, and I will probably never have the opportunity to "repay" them, but I can pay it forward by helping others when situations present themselves.

We're all stretched to the max right now. We're doing way too much with way too little each day, making far too little money, and we're stretching ourselves to the breaking point. So how can we make the time to pay it forward, and where will we find the energy?

Let's look at a few ways we can pay it forward. First, Christmastime is a time of total extravagance and commercialism for most of us. Do we really need to give each other all that stuff that we can't afford to give and that collects dust anyway, or would some of that money help bring a lot of sunshine into someone else's dreary existence?

When I was a teenager, my family established a long-standing tradition, one we observed until my mother's death. Instead of giving each other expensive gifts, we pooled our money and threw a huge Christmas Eve party for family, friends, neighbors, and friends of friends who had no place to spend Christmas Eve. We didn't serve a few light refreshments; we served enough to feed an army, and everyone was offered a "to-go" bag when they left. We made many new friends through this party, and we looked forward to the next one all year long. The party was our present to each other. No gift meant more to any member of my family than the party did.

One Christmas, in addition to the party, my mother and I decided to round up $500 in groceries for two people we knew were in dire need. We figured that $500 would buy about six months' worth of groceries if we shopped frugally, bought the store brand, and used coupons—it would fill their freezer, refrigerator, and pantry. Back then, Kroger packaged their discount store brand in white labels with ginormous, ugly black letters. You could spot these cans and packages a mile away. Mother said, "Oh my, we can't go during the day. If anyone sees us with all these store brands, they'll think we're in dire straits." So off we went to Kroger at midnight.

We filled three grocery carts to overflowing, and when we headed for the checkout line, we ran into a member of our church. We were horrified. We said a very quick hello, avoiding eye contact, and headed straight to a line at the other end of the store. On the way home, we laughed until our stomachs hurt.

My brother knew he was going to deliver our little surprise, but when he saw what we had bought, he wanted to strangle us. He suggested that perhaps we might like to call a moving van! My mother and I had so much fun doing this, and the recipients were thrilled.

You can't do this kind of thing all the time, but you will never know the reward of doing something until you do it. For some reason, the less you can afford to do something grand, the more joy it brings you.

You can also do many small things to brighten another person's day. You can entertain a friend's children on a weekend afternoon to give the parents time to work in the yard or take time off to relax. Let the kids bring their iPads, and ask them to help you bake chocolate chip cookies. Explore Pinterest or YouTube with them. Hey, it keeps you young and in touch with pop culture.

One day, when Dylan was spending the weekend with me, and we wanted to find out what people stationed in Antarctica did in their spare time; we came across a New Year's festival called Icestock. When I said something like, "You know, like Woodstock," he looked at me as if I had two heads. He had never heard of Woodstock! You just never know how entertaining paying it forward can be until you try it.

You can care for a neighbor's pet while they're out of town so the pet doesn't have to be shipped off to a kennel. You can visit infirmed neighbors, bring them an occasional dinner, run errands for them, or just surprise them with flowers.

There are as many ways to pay it forward as there are individuals. I never knew that paying it forward would come back to me. I never dreamed of taking this kind of help from friends and strangers, but I was sure thankful for their help when it arrived. Now I have to remember to keep paying it forward.

There's a saying that goes, "When the student is ready, the teacher will appear." Now that I'm focused on how I can help someone through a miserable time, the perfect opportunity has landed at my doorstep. I spent a little more than a decade in New York, with a little time in Long Beach. Parts of Long Island have been devastated by Hurricane Sandy, and Long Beach was one of the hardest-hit areas on Long Island. Would you believe that my ground-floor apartment was destroyed by Hurricane Sandy? And my friends and former landlords live upstairs in that house.

Somehow, some way, I hope to find my way to Long Beach to help those in need before their recovery is complete, which will take years. In the meantime, I check in with my friends from time to time, and we share disaster stories. It's not often you can say, "I understand," and really mean it, but this is one instance where I really do understand. I've earned the t-shirt.

These days, I find serious undergraduate and graduate students with little to no budget, and I edit their papers for a fraction of my normal fees when time permits. Today's kids couldn't possibly work their way through school the way we did, and they'll be indentured servants for life. I enjoy learning about their interests. Sometimes, I'm fascinated; other times, I'm appalled, but it's another way to keep up with what's going on out in the world. We both benefit from it, so it's a win-win opportunity.

PART III

MELISSA – THE RESCUE PROFESSIONAL
AND CRISIS COUNSELOR

HEART THE CCP

As a fire and rescue professional, I was accustomed to short-term assignments. In this case, I couldn't go home at the end of the day—this WAS home, so there was no place to escape. Further, this was a long-term recovery; and survivors qualified for crisis counseling. A state that has been declared a federal disaster also qualifies for Individual Assistance (IA). That state can apply for a FEMA Crisis Counseling Program (CCP) grant to provide counseling services or emotional support to survivors. This would be the first large-scale implementation of this program in Tennessee.

I received a call from a local mental health agency asking if I was interested in working on this grant program as a team leader.

I said, "Yes." I didn't know it at the time, but it would become one of the most meaningful, humbling, and experiential jobs I have ever held.

Under this grant, crisis counselors would go into the community and meet with survivors wherever they happen to be—at homes, hotels, motels, trailers, tents, schools, workplaces, streets, etc., providing emotional support and resource referrals.

No two days were ever alike, because no two survivors were ever alike. The key to a successful crisis-counseling program is to see every survivor as an individual—similar experience, different response, but life's like that, isn't it?

Imagine being able to go out into the community, knock on survivors' doors, and if they were willing, have them tell their life stories. Humbling! I definitely learned more about hope, resiliency, and courage from each of them than I was able to share. I was there to talk about coping skills. The irony was that they were living it; they were coping. You could have an entire neighborhood of homes that experienced the same amount of water in each home, and each, even within the same household, would have a different reaction and coping skill set. That is life at its essence, isn't it? There isn't an itinerary that tells us what will happen and when it will happen in this life. There isn't a road map showing how to negotiate those things when they do happen. We have experts, we have theorists, we have books, videos, stories, and traditions, but the reality is that we learn by experience, and there is so much to be experienced that no amount of it can prepare us for it all.

I have been blessed to meet crisis counselors and program leaders from across the United States, and each of them shares the same passion and humility that comes from walking with others along the road of rescue and recovery when hearts are raw, tender, and vulnerable. This is one program that truly touches the lives of others and assists in recovery and healing like no other I've seen to date. One reason that it can be so effective is that in some cases, it can last up to one to two years. This means that crisis counselors who work with these survivors on an extended basis can develop relationships and participate in the healing process, often witnessing the survivors' restoration to their new normal.

The service is confidential. It does not record personal information on anyone. Anonymous reports showing emotional events categorized by demographic is all that is maintained on file. This allows the program to see at a glance how the population is coping, what extra resources may be needed, and how to best serve the survivors on their road to recovery. Equally important, the trends in event reactions to the disaster can serve as justification for a program's extension. (As an example, at the six-month mark, Nashville had more known completed suicides than were reported in New Orleans at the six-month mark following Hurricane Katrina.) By "known," I mean what was reported to the program; we do not know how many went unreported or unknown.

The CCP was an extended boots-on-the-ground program, and we could go back to the Volunteer Organizations Active in Disasters (VOADS) months later and let them know which areas still needed assistance rebuilding, etc.

Survivors appreciated the FEMA recovery grants (the max grant was $29,900), but they were insufficient to cover the entire expense of rebuilding their homes. True to form, Nashville's own stepped up to the plate to fill in the gap. Garth Brooks, for example, raised millions for survivors through a series of benefit concerts. The United Methodist Church Committee on Relief (UMCOR), and the Community Foundation put together a scholarship for survivors to cover their emotional support needs. Up to 250 survivors were eligible for the scholarship and only had to share their first name and last initial to protect confidentiality.

The CCP program and other agencies could recommend individual survivors, first responders, and/or aid workers for a scholarship. The survivor could see any counselor of his or her choosing at no charge for at least a year, including in-patient services, and/or medications as needed. This was an incredible asset made possibly through the generosity of so many.

This is definitely THE program to emulate. It SAVES LIVES! In essence, this program kicks in where the CCP leaves off. CCP may bring someone a long way through their healing journey, but if they don't quite reach their destination, this program can carry them all the way home. By funding professional counseling, survivors could use their personal funds to rebuild their homes and take care of their families. Honestly, when faced with needing a roof and a counselor, people will choose a roof every time at the expense of their emotional health. This program allowed access to emotional health support, and it worked. It worked. It worked! It saved lives and mitigated years of suffering.

As a first responder, I hadn't realized all that I had been missing in regard to long-term recovery efforts. When the sirens wind down and the vehicles return to the station, the work is far from over. People have emotional needs that linger. Seeing a community rebuild from its raw state to its state of new normal gives you a new appreciation for the intricacies of the process. It's nothing like what you see on the news. It's a long, hard, dirty, exhausting process.

The news might depict a neighborhood all shiny and new with dry, fresh paint, new keys, and that looks just fine. But what about the people in that neighborhood? Actually, the emotional recovery may be just beginning. It might continue for another year, or 10, or a lifetime.

I make it a practice now to encourage others to make the time to reach out to friends or family members who have survived a disaster and ask them how they are doing. It can mitigate the isolation they feel; it can help support them as they struggle with emotional issues that often lag behind, due to physical rebuilding needs, and so many other things that often postpone the healing process.

Our society is so driven by social media and news that often when an event disappears from the TV or Internet headlines, we think all is well. That isn't the case, and the survivors are still struggling to recover long after the next disaster takes over the headlines. For example, survivors in West Tennessee were still struggling to recover from the Thousand-Year Flood when they were hit by tornadoes and the Mississippi River flooding to levels never before seen. This meant that flood survivors from 2010 were also impacted by tornadoes in 2011, and a majority of those who flooded in West Tennessee in 2010 flooded again in 2011. Can you imagine their emotional stress from repeated disasters?

The new disasters resulted in Tennessee receiving two more CCP grants. I worked in the field on both grants as the state coordinator for the 2011 CCP program, traveling extensively and saw the program offer its services to both new and repeat disaster survivors. At one point, Tennessee was working three separate CCP grants at the same time. Many of the staff from 2010 rolled into the new grants in 2011. The CCP workers labored tirelessly and selflessly for over two straight years in the field supporting survivors and sharing in their stories of both suffering and triumph. These workers deserve a commendation! I know my life has been changed forever for the better through my work with them. If you ever get a chance to sit and talk with one of them and listen to their experiences in your own state (without names or places of course), do it!

SANTA, THE TOOTH FAIRY, AND THE EASTER BUNNY

I learned long ago in a psychology class that all behavior is purposeful. I have come to believe this to be true. It can explain a myriad of actions in others as well as in ourselves. Its application to disaster relief work is valuable. Disaster survivors typically have no experiential baseline, and they are at a loss to explain how they feel.

As a crisis counselor, you are working to some extent as a behavioral health catastrophic scene investigator (CSI). You have just a few moments to assess how someone is doing and how best to help them. This same concept works to gain insight into your own behavior that you might not be consciously aware of.

As an example, why are you suddenly shopping more than normal, drinking more alcohol, eating junk food, or sleeping more? Is it an effort to self-sooth? Is it an effort to avoid the present reality that is currently overwhelming? Are you snapping at people before they even finish their sentence as a form of self-protection because you cannot handle criticism? Are you having somatic symptoms like chest pains, headaches, stomach issues, etc., because it is overwhelmed emotionally and you do not yet know how to ask for help?

In our society, emotional issues are a stigma and are seen as weakness. Oftentimes, we try to cover them up or say that everything is "fine." Think about this the next time someone says, "I'm 'fine.'" Fine can often be code to mean the person is feeling **F**'d up, **I**nsecure, **N**eurotic, or **E**xplosive. (Feel free to add other descriptive adjectives that start with those letters.) When we are good, we say "good." If we feel physically sick, we say so. But when people are overwhelmed emotionally, they will often answer, "Fine," when in fact, they are hurting a great deal inside.

Think of the times you or a loved one has used that term. Sometimes you really are fine; other times, when it's nothing more than a polite reply, you may not be fine at all. In this instance, why not use it as a clue to dig a little deeper. You might want to ask some follow-up questions or check in with a friend or family member of the survivor. It's important to respect people's boundaries and privacy and trust that they are much more "expert" in themselves than you can be. You're a professional; let your discernment guide you. Even if you're a layperson, you can sense when you're reached the line and need to back off.

All behavior is purposeful, even our own. When we cannot understand or express emotion ourselves, our behavior does it for us. Study those around you, specifically how they are acting. Think about how you have acted in the last few days. It can give insight into the actual reason behind the behavior, and this can help you understand others' behavior.

Let me give you an example that hits close to home. It took me a long time to work on the chapters of this book, far longer than my cohorts wanted. Why? Why did I find myself wanting to clean the house or perform any other onerous task rather than sitting down to work on my writing? I came to discover it was because I would have to sit down and relive a time that was difficult and painful. It was uncomfortable to write about those events. Once I understood that, I was able to write about the events.

Once I figured out what I was afraid of, reliving the sadness of shared loss and suffering, and allowing myself to feel that way, I realized how very powerful a growth experience it had been. I could then embrace sitting quietly and reliving those moments in the hope of paying forward some of the lessons that I learned from our shared disaster experience here in Tennessee. Disasters that touch our lives are part of our journey, a journey that enriches us, and a journey that changes us on a journey that never ends.

Many people are raised to believe in a fair and just world. We are taught that if we work hard and do the right things, we'll be rewarded. Sadly, somewhere along the line, the rules changed, or we discovered the truth: Santa doesn't fit down the chimney, the Tooth Fairy is broke, and the Easter Bunny doesn't lay eggs. It's important to learn those things so that we see life as it really is. Still, it's important to be hopeful and optimistic, to believe in good, to want the best that life has to offer. There's nothing wrong with guarded optimism. That way, you're following Plan A, but you're aware that you may have to implement Plan B, even if you don't know what Plan B is yet.

If we keep thinking that we have lived correctly, so 'this' shouldn't have happened to us, we will remain stuck in that position until we change our thinking, and the former is a very painful position in which to dwell. Let's face it: bad things do happen to good people. Thinking we have earned a good life by following the 'good person' rules makes it hard to process our feelings when it all goes horribly wrong. Once we can accept that the world isn't always warm and fuzzy, then we can rise against it, and move forward with purpose.

Once we accept this, we can receive the good times, the joyous moments, and the gift of quiet moments with a deep sense of gratitude. Good times, therefore, become like treasures, as we no longer expect but accept them freely when received.

I am grateful for even the quietest moments, because they provide me with the opportunity to recharge. By recharging, I have the reserve to be entirely present with another person who is going through a rough time. Recognizing that life is hard sometimes, I can fully support someone in their recovery without judging or having to find a reason why this occurred to them. Sometimes there is no reason.

Suppose you have an automobile accident. Does it really matter whether you were hit by a Nissan or a Ford truck? Of course not. Accept that it happened and that it sucked. Now focus on your recovery.

Eventually, everyone experiences some type of loss. It may not be a natural disaster, but crisis visits everyone with a pulse. No one is immune, even if it seems that way. We may be just a moment from our next disaster. Isn't it best if we can learn to enjoy the peacefulness and health that we have in the moment, since nothing is guaranteed? That makes the current moment even more meaningful because we can fully appreciate it.

Besides, some of the most genuine people I know are those who have survived periods of great suffering. Why? Because they know firsthand, that life can present hard and cruel moments, that it's unpredictable. Experiencing darker days has a way of magnifying the joy in the brighter days.

Suppose you ate only food prepared by a four-star chef. You would love food, but exquisite food would be your baseline for comparison. Now imagine that you grew up in a slum and foraged for food in a dumpster. Suddenly one day, you were invited into a brand new home, and you ate a meal prepared by a four-star chef. You would have a spectrum of experience for comparison, and you would be even more enriched by and appreciative of the new exquisite food. This holds true to our emotional lives. And each of us has an emotional life if we are brave enough to experience it. The more we can experience within ourselves, and the more we can be present to help others when they are hurting, the more enriched our lives can become. Live bravely. Live exquisitely. Allow yourself to feel and be present in all the emotion that is around you.

It helps to look at any disaster, crisis, or loss that touches our lives as a necessary part of our life journey. I will remember the flood and the people who courageously shared their stories with me for the rest of my life. I am a better person for these experiences. We each carry forward the sum total of our experiences, whether we are survivors, responders, supporters or a mixture of these. All of our behavior is purposeful… all of our experiences invaluable.

HEART CONNECTIONS

During a time of crisis, you meet some of the best people in the world (and unfortunately, some of the worst too). Two of the best people I know, I met during the aftermath of the flood. I first met MJ at a weekly coffee meeting at a Bellevue café. She was with a group of her friends from River Plantation Section X. Without any instruction from the "outside," this group of remarkable women had developed their own recovery team and were supporting one another every step of the way and updating each other weekly on new developments.

While sitting with them during one of their weekly meetings I remember that my ears perked up particularly when I heard MJ say that she had been a flight attendant for TWA. I have been a pilot since 1995, and as a result, I felt a connection to her, and I wanted to get to know her better and to learn more about her time with the airlines. I didn't get a chance to talk with her at length during the first months of the program, but I was impressed each week with the strength and knowledge that she brought and displayed in the group meetings. I would come to know her well in the months to come.

A few months after the flood, the United Methodist Committee on Relief (UMCOR) applied for and received an emotional health grant from the Community Foundation. This was a landmark idea. It was very difficult to connect survivors with professional emotional support. First, as I stated earlier, when faced with rebuilding a kitchen or seeing a "shrink," most people opt for sink vs. shrink. Secondly, when their income reached a certain level, they did not qualify for free counseling. Lastly, those who did qualify could expect to wait up to four to eight weeks to meet with someone.

Imagine breaking your arm, being in severe pain, and being told that it would be eight weeks before you could get an appointment with an ER doctor. It was heartbreaking and frustrating to see people who needed and wanted professional help but could not get it.

When UMCOR appeared, it was an answer to prayer. Seriously, this was a brilliant, lifesaving measure. However, fantastic as it was, there remained some gaps in service. Some survivors needed and wanted emotional support but lacked the funds, means, or ability to leave home to get to a counselor. I had an idea to bridge the gap by bringing the counselor to them. The trouble was finding someone who was willing to go out into the field to counsel others. I asked a well-respected, licensed co-worker whom she could recommend.

She introduced me to Pam Kaufman, and the rest is history. Pam has a charismatic charm about her that makes her relatable to others. She was also willing to travel to the survivor to help them, and she speaks fluent Spanish. The first few survivors I introduced her to loved her and recommended her to their friends in need of counseling. Before long, Pam was playing an integral role in going to survivors' homes and helping them recover from their emotional flood damage. She made it possible to reach the segment of those impacted by the disaster who wouldn't have received professional emotional support otherwise. Pam was a lifesaver.

As the role of UMCOR evolved to take on more case management, they hired me to serve both as a case manager and as an emotional/spiritual counselor. Now I was able to help survivors rebuild physically as well as emotionally. We were assigned to the Bellevue area, so I was able to reconnect with survivors I already knew from the Tennessee Recovery Project who were still having a difficult time rebuilding.

I got back in touch with MJ to check on her, and through the work of these organizations, we were able to help her rebuild. In turn, MJ referred us to her friends in need of help, and we were all able to network together to help restore parts of the community. Often I would stop by to say hello to MJ, and we would share stories over coffee. Our friendship blossomed as she told me stories of her time with the airlines, her freelance writing, her 'big, not so fat Greek family,' and her cats. MJ, along the way, had asked for someone to assist with the emotional recovery of survivors in her area. I introduced her to Pam, and they became friends as MJ helped connect Pam with survivors who needed professional emotional support. Over time we would all meet together to check in on each other's lives.

Over coffee one day, MJ, Pam, and I toyed with the idea of writing about lessons learned from the Tennessee floods from three unique perspectives—that of a renegade survivor, a seasoned recovery worker, and a licensed family counselor who makes house calls. Together, almost three years after the flood and two years after starting this project, this work is a compilation of our experiences, mistakes, and triumphs.

It is a bond of friendship born from disaster. I have gained two invaluable friends for life from the trials faced by all of us courtesy of the Tennessee floods.

SHHH! BEST KEPT SECRET

Now that I have your attention, this secret actually needs to be broadcast far and wide. I have worked in emergency services for over two decades, and I had never heard of FEMAs Crisis Counseling Program (CCP) until the 2010 floods in Tennessee. I want to share the program with you here briefly. In my opinion, it is one of the best programs ever to come out of FEMA, and when implemented, it saves lives and reduces emotional pain in survivors. It is not widely known, but hopefully that is changing—and quickly. With your help, we can spread the news to the far corners of the country and beyond.

The FEMA CCP is a program for which the state can apply if a federal disaster reaches the level of individual assistance (IA). If survivors are allowed to receive monetary assistance from FEMA and apply for Small Business Administration (SBA) loans, then the state is also eligible to apply for a CCP program for the disaster. (SBA is not really the best term for the loan program because it creates ALL kinds of confusion among individuals who read the words and think they are not a business so they cannot apply. That needs to be better explained to the public. It prevented some survivors from applying for aid because they assumed it was for businesses only.) More importantly, many people don't understand that numerous programs offering assistance require applicants to make an application with the SBA before applying for other assistance.

I hope you made it through the above paragraphs of acronyms and explanations without falling asleep. Stay with me here; this is important! The CCP program exists to work with survivors to teach them the skills they need to grow from their experiences as they make their way through the aftermath of a disaster. It is set up so that CCP workers are not required to have a mental health license. It is not intended to provide professional counseling in the field. If a survivor needs those services, the CCP workers are trained to refer them for professional care. CCP workers are trained in psychological first aid, skills for psychological recovery, and skill sets needed to work with survivors during particular phases of a disaster.

In a nutshell, CCP workers are trained to go out into the field, go door to door, and sit and talk with you, to listen to whatever is on your mind, and to give you tips and fundamental skills to reduce any emotional pain you are experiencing. Often, current tragedy brings up past tragedy. So in surviving a disaster, it can trigger other difficult events and losses that you have experienced in your life. The CCP workers are trained to listen to whatever is being shared at that given time, even if it does not feel disaster related. What is important is that connections can be made, painful memories can be shared and released, and resiliency can be fostered.

From a survivor's perspective, one of the best parts of the CCP program is that it records NO identifiable information. The CCP workers never record names or addresses. Further, they are trained to keep the information you share with them confidential (i.e., they won't leave your home, go next door, and tell Mrs. Jones that you are having the same emotions she is describing, etc.). The only time a CCP worker would ever share your information is if you threaten to harm yourself or someone else; and then, like any other care worker, they are obligated to ask a professional to come in and help keep you safe. Even if this occurs, the CCP program does not record any personal information.

CCP workers do fill out data sheets—but these sheets contain no recognizable personal information. They ask for simple demographics such as the age range of the survivors, where they were seen (in home settings or businesses and the zip codes of the settings). You are no more identifiable than that. It also asks general questions about what survivors are dealing with; for example, are they sad, are they having trouble sleeping, and have they been offered the proper resources.

There is absolutely no way to track down a specific survivor from the information on the form. It simply allows the program and FEMA to spot the trends in the survivor population. It shows trends by age range, setting, etc., in order to tailor help for a given population or demographic struggling with particular issues. It also helps justify a program extension if a significant portion of the population is still working to recover emotionally.

If you live in an area affected by a disaster and are looking for one of the most rewarding jobs you will ever have, contact your state mental health office, and ask how to apply to work with the CCP program in your area. You will spend the next three to 12 months going door to door, hearing stories from every walk of life, and witnessing for yourself the strength of the human spirit. There is no other opportunity that will allow you to learn so much from others in such a short time. As you help survivors recover from their emotional pain, you will get far more from them than you can give. This job will change you by giving you a fresh perspective on life, and you'll come away from your experiences changed forever.

As a CCP worker, you play the role of ambassador in another significant way. With the stigma still attached to mental health in our country, survivors are often terrified to admit they are hurting emotionally. However, once you build a rapport with survivors and they experience relief just by talking about their feelings, they begin to heal, and you have helped shatter the myth that mental health is taboo. It's a grassroots program, sans diagnostic terms and forms to fill out (in triplicate, no less). What a painless and easy way to make help available. It may not be the ending point, but it's a great starting point.

I have been blessed to work many types of jobs over the years. Hands down, working with the CCP program has been the most fulfilling and inspiring job I have ever held. It better prepared me for coping with the next disaster to strike in my own life by seeing how others had handled disaster in their own. It is by far, one of, if not the best, life-saving, suffering-reducing programs FEMA has instituted for responding to disasters.

WHAT STOPS THE HURT?

If you jumped to this chapter out of order, it means you are likely hurting and in need of support and comfort. I wish I had a magic-potion remedy for you. The truth is, the answer is different for everyone. Each of us brings our unique life experiences with us when facing crisis and disaster. In America, we tend to hide the truth that life is hard, and we do so very well. Many of us are raised to believe that life will be relatively easy, and that if you work hard, you will get what you deserve. Once we grow into adulthood, we discover, most often through experiencing tragedy, that life is not necessarily easy even for the most deserving. I have found that life is better when approached differently. I live now in what I guess would be called a guarded optimistic state—hoping for the best, recognizing that hard times will likely come.

I have spent time with family members who have lost a loved one to suicide after a disaster. The disaster wasn't the precise cause, but it was a contributing factor. We lost survivors to suicide in each of the last three disasters in Tennessee. Data collected during the 2010 floods showed that Nashville had a higher (known) suicide rate at the six-month, post-disaster mark than New Orleans did after Hurricane Katrina. You probably did not know that because it wasn't a widely publicized statistic. However, it was a heartbreaking reality of the 2010 floods. Unfortunately, suicides also occurred among survivors in our subsequent floods and tornadoes the following year. They are also occurring at an all-time high among our returning military personnel. And suicide ranks among the top 10 causes of death in America annually. You likely feel uncomfortable even reading this because discussing mental health is still far too taboo.

We need to get over that. The only way to help each other through difficult times is to acknowledge the elephant in the room—to acknowledge that each of us processes emotional pain differently. We need to learn to feel empathy toward our friends and loved ones who may be hurting. If two different people suffer the same burn on their arms, they may react in two completely different ways based upon their genetic makeup, background, and overall pain tolerance. The same holds true for emotional pain.

What cripples one person may not even slow down someone else. Each experience is unique to the individual. If a tragic event occurs, people WILL hurt emotionally. They may hurt that same day, or in some cases, it may take several years, but the individual will process the event at some point.

Make a point to ask how a survivor, a survivor of anything—loss, disaster, or crisis is feeling emotionally. We all know someone. Let them know that you want to hear what they have to say, and that you will not judge them. Let them sense that you feel empathy. Let them know you will not see them as weak for being human and for responding emotionally to a life-changing event. Destigmatizing emotional health will help all of us walk through life's tragedies better as will supporting others during their time of need.

Just because you are hurting emotionally after a disaster does NOT mean you will contemplate suicide. You may never contemplate suicide. On the other hand, there may be times when people are so overwhelmed from a disaster and from what they have dealt with in life prior to the disaster that suicide may seem to be their only means of escaping the crippling pain they feel. Don't be afraid to reach out, encourage, and talk about whatever is on their mind. You may be able to help guide them to seek professional help if they need it. And don't worry—you can't "catch" suicide from talking about it with someone, but you may very well prevent it from occurring.

Whether it is relatively tolerable emotional pain or severe emotional pain, a common denominator that helps to reduce the pain is feeling connected to someone. Isolation magnifies emotional pain. If you can check in on friends, family members, and neighbors after a disaster and encourage them to talk about how they are doing, you can help to reduce their pain—especially once the news coverage of the story fades and it seems that the town has moved on.

The average time to recover emotionally after a disaster is three to five YEARS. That means that even now, in 2013, some survivors of the 2010 floods may be just starting to heal emotionally, or some may even be several years from completing their healing process. There is no timeline to healing; it is as individual as each survivor is. Keep reaching out, keep asking, keep remembering what they have experienced, and do not be afraid to talk to them about any part of the emotional process, no matter how dark or scary. Being present with them is the greatest gift that you can give to help them rebuild their resiliency, hope, and courage—and helping someone to overcome a difficult time in life is a gift that you give yourself as well.

R & R: REST AND RENEWAL FOR THE CAREGIVER

You got it; this is about compassion fatigue—aka, secondhand trauma. If you're a recovery worker or a first responder, you may think, "I don't need to worry about this; I'm just fine." That may or may not be true, but humor me, and let's assume the latter.

If you're a caregiver, it probably goes against your nature to take time for yourself when working a disaster. You may think you don't have it bad, especially when comparing your life to the lives of the survivors. You may think you have your entire life in order. You may be absolutely correct, for this finite moment—this snapshot in time.

Now I can't predict tomorrow, and I am pretty sure no one else can either. Compassionate care is as important for the compassion caregivers as it is for the compassion care receivers (survivors). You have to take care of yourself habitually, whether living everyday, routine life or working a disaster, whether it's your own or someone else's disaster. We are never guaranteed tomorrow, but if there is a tomorrow and that tomorrow brings crisis, we may need that little extra bit of reserve strength.

If you look at past disasters, you will find numerous examples of how hard life is on people affected by the disaster. For example, a number of the flood survivors in West Tennessee who made it through the 2010 floods, flooded AGAIN less than one year later when the Mississippi River reached historic flood levels. Tornado survivors in 2011, some of whom had just completed rebuilding, experienced another tornado just DAYS after rebuilding, and the second tornado destroyed their homes AGAIN a second time less than a year later in 2012. You will find examples of cancer survivors who beat the odds only to die in a flood or a tornado. You will never hear that Uncle Joe, who lost his leg in the war, was disaster proof because he had already suffered a terrible misfortune. This is the reason we must always work to keep our resilience up for the next emergency even while we face a current one. We have no idea what lurks around the next corner.

Everyone working a disaster soon learns they must pace themselves. During the flood recovery work, it felt like we were in a marathon, and then suddenly, our finish line got pushed back several more miles (months) by both an extension to the FEMA CCP program and the creation of the UMCOR case management program. Many who faced the end of the disaster recovery cycle continued to work for another three to 12 months.

In addition, we were hit in our state by another round of floods and tornadoes, which led to two more federal disaster declarations. Crisis counselors in West and Southeast Tennessee would go on to work an incredible 27 months straight. Because these things are unpredictable, we must set healthy boundaries at all times, making time for rest and relaxation so that we have sufficient compassion and strength in reserve and so that we are never completely wiped out physically and/or emotionally.

How do we do this? First, it's no secret that whether you're recovering or working to recover others, you're under stress; what you may not realize at the time is that stress is cumulative. The longer the recovery period, the more critical self-care becomes to maintain health and resiliency. There are many excellent books, websites, courses, and videos on self-care. Fire up your Internet search engine, research the various methods of self-care, and find what works best for YOU.

There is no one-size-fits-all "best practice" for remaining healthy and strong in the face of adversity. Find what fits your lifestyle and incorporate it into your routine. Make the time to do a little extra of whatever it is during disaster recovery. (This, of course, refers to healthy endeavors. Self-medication, such as overindulging in alcohol, is not considered good self-care, so don't become a permanent fixture in your favorite watering hole and quote this chapter.)

A way to think about stress during disaster recovery is this: You are wearing your favorite black shirt and black jeans over to a friend's house to spend the day. Once you get there, you realize your friend has four solid white German shepherds and five gray cats living in the house. (No worries—this isn't a chapter on animal hoarders.) The more time you spend moving around in the home, the more animal hair you will accumulate all over you and your clothes. At some point, even if you are not allergic to the animals in the beginning, as your clothes accumulate hair, you may begin to sneeze and itch. Unless you go outside, brush off the pet hair, and temporarily change your environment, you can become overwhelmed by allergies you didn't even know you had. Just seeing the accumulation of animal hair all over you can become a distraction from enjoying the time you spend with your friend.

And so it is with disaster recovery. You need a break. Schedule regular breaks or take them when the opportunity arises—whether it's a weekend getaway; allowing yourself a long, hot bath with a favorite book at night; a double shot with "whip" from your favorite coffeehouse; a good laugh with a friend—whatever it is that helps reduce your stress. Make sure to take time to build those activities into your day and into your week. It will allow you to decompress, gain invaluable perspective, and return to work renewed and better able to focus on those you are serving.

"That is all well and good," you say, "but what if I am the one recovering from the disaster?" It is even more important for you to build in some type of breaks for yourself, whatever "break" means to you. Some people might even schedule a weekend getaway to visit a friend or just for a change of scenery. For others, a break might simply mean taking the time to talk with a friend.

Some people find it easier to talk with someone they don't know. During the 2010 flood, FEMA and the Substance Abuse and Mental Health Services Administration (SAMHSA) realized the need for 24/7 emotional support and created the Disaster Distress Helpline. Anyone—survivor, recovery worker, first responder—can call or text this number day or night and reach a caring, compassionate person. **Anyone can reach free help 24/7 at 1.800.985.5990 or text "talk with us" to 66746.**

The most important action you can take to recover yourself or others is to take time to relax and renew your body, mind, and spirit. There are few things as important in disaster recovery as this single act. Rest and renewal can greatly assist your ability to recover from this disaster and to prepare yourself better for what comes next.

PART IV

PAM – THE FAMILY GRIEF COUNSELOR

COME HELL AND HIGH WATER...BUT NOT NECESSARILY IN THAT ORDER

The weeks following the flood were hell for so many! Of course, my hell wasn't flood related, as was the case for thousands of Nashvillians whose hell came with the high waters. For these people it was about the loss of homes, material possessions, priceless heirlooms, pets, control, order, the known and familiar—even human life. Life for them, whatever it was before the flood, was, well, "fine." Then, like a bad dream, it wasn't fine anymore.

As with all trauma survivors, people's reactions were as varied as the people experiencing them were—hyperactivity, lethargy, numbness, confusion, profound sadness, anger, cognitive disorientation, etc. To make matters worse, because it was a mass disaster, there was the need to share private loss publically and with strangers for the most part. To complicate matters further, there was the issue of survivor guilt. "Why did my neighbor, my friend lose everything? It seemed to pass right over me, but wow! They lost everything!"

Come Hell AND High Water... But Not Necessarily in That Order – Pam

The disaster relief workers did an excellent job of picking up the physical pieces and helping people begin to rebuild their lives. Needed just as badly, if not more so, were emotional relief workers to pick up the emotional pieces. You can build a new home and put someone back in it, but if you don't help that person make sense of what has happened, don't give them a way to grieve the old house that had meaning, value, significance, memories, laughter, and tears in the walls, they will struggle to find peace in that new home. People needed counseling. I knew that because I AM a counselor. I hoped they were getting it somewhere. I needed a counselor myself, so help sure as heck wasn't going to come from me.

HAPPY NEW YEAR?

As America ushered in 2011, I was pleased to leave the pain of 2010 behind, at least some of it. Truth is, some of it followed me into the New Year. Truth is, I really hadn't made much progress in my adjustment to life in Tennessee. Every morning I woke up wishing I had awakened to that beautiful California sunshine, MY beautiful California sunshine. Of course, it didn't help that it was the worst winter in years according to the experts—the weather people, and too, my neighbors.

I hadn't made much progress in my bank account either, and this was of concern. The move to Tennessee had wiped us out—foreclosure, credit card debt, old cars with car payments, no savings, and massive income reduction for the last three quarters of 2010. I was hopeful 2011 would be a turnaround year. I took a leap of faith and leased a new private practice office in Brentwood, one of the most upscale cities in the Nashville metropolitan area. Following the *'Field of Dreams'* model, I decided to believe that if I opened a practice, "they" would come, "they" meaning clients. My website was up and running, I was advertising on a national locator, and I was passing out business cards like a politician seeking reelection. I had a few clients, but not nearly enough to keep my practice open.

Just when I had all but given up, the call came. It was late one Tuesday night in early March. "This is the Tennessee Recovery Project, we have a female flood survivor, she's in bad shape... suicidal... and mobile crisis won't meet with her for a psychiatric evaluation. Can you see her at her place of residence? We think she's dissociating...."

"Excuse me...," I inquire, "Who are you, how did you get my name? And, are you telling me there are still people nearly a year later who are not housed, still not OK?"

"My name is Melissa Riley. I got your name from one of the mental health workers you met at the Opryland Hotel layoff [when the hotel was closed due to flood damage] last year. She thought you might be willing to help," she responded.

"I can't get to her until late tonight, maybe 8:00 p.m., but I will be there." And I was. That night I saw the first of over 30 flood recovery survivors that I have been blessed with the privilege of working with, helping, knowing. That night was the beginning of a working relationship with the Tennessee Recovery Project. My services were paid by a grant for mental health by the partnership between UMCOR and the Community Foundation, which on a purely selfish note, has turned my practice upside down and my bank account right side up. Had people told me I would have moved to Tennessee in this lifetime, I would have told them they were crazy! Had anyone told me I would live through a major flood three weeks after that move, I would have said double crazy. And had anyone told me that the move and that flood would be my saving grace, I would never have believed it!

The place I disdained, the thing I had feared had rescued me!

(Note: You will be pleased to know that at the time of this writing over two years later, I am enjoying my newfound life in Tennessee; that, in fact, I am even telling my family and friends in California that they should consider moving here! No, I don't say much about the tornados. Why spoil a good sales pitch?)

BUILDING BRIDGES OVER TROUBLED WATERS

As my work with flood survivors began to unfold, it became apparent that those struggling most in their recovery had issues deeper than the highest flood line marker. People came in with the flood as their headline story, but once we got past the front page, it was the story hidden away in obscure sections and columns that required closer examination. Those were the real stories, and they were sometimes hard to find. They were stories about unhappy marriages, unresolved losses, broken relationships between parents and children, complex health issues, and the betrayal of marital infidelity. Many had inadequate support systems and others had long histories of having been disenfranchised and marginalized for some reason from family and/or society. Many had been re-victimized by the very people entrusted to help them recover—the flood recovery program itself. There were far too many people dealing with stolen or trashed possessions, substandard building, and contractor abandonment.

The clients came in broken, some in smaller, more fragile pieces than others, but all broken. Now, fortunately, all finally were getting the counseling support they had never received for lack of money, time, resources—who knows? They were long overdue. It was time, time to build some bridges over troubled waters. I am only one of the mental health professionals privileged to work with these amazingly resilient people. There are many other stories, many other people whose stories I have not had the privilege of sharing. As for my thirty-something survivors, I promised them, I promised myself that I would share some important things they have to say, on their behalf, kind of a Survivor Survey Says.

Survivor Survey Says

1. Know who is on your "stretcher squad" before you need one. Cultivate and list your support system: Who to call for help, where to get advice. Put a list together of your 'go to' people. Keep it in your wallet, purse, car, lock box.
2. Work on life's issues as they arise—don't delay, don't deny. Complexity is compounded by a disaster.
3. Keep valuables and irreplaceable items off-site—in a storage unit, with a friend, in a safe deposit box. Make copies of important documents and store safely.
4. Put together a survival kit—what do you absolutely need if you can't grab much and time is of the essence—spare eye glasses, prescriptions, keys, cell phone, etc.
5. Restore familiarity and normalcy as quickly as is healthy for you—establish a routine. We all function better with some predictability and a measure of control over our daily activities.

6. Be nice to yourself. Your loss is your loss, even if someone else's is "bigger." Remember, too, that your reaction to loss isn't always commensurate or in direct proportion to the loss itself. There are factors such as timing, circumstances, and multiplicity to take into consideration.
7. There is no right or wrong way to "do" this, just your way. You will process and heal your own way in your own time. Do get help if you need it, and make sure you feel comfortable with the mental health professional you are working with. You truly are your own best healer, and although a professional can help, you are the expert on you.
8. Don't place too much value on things; simplicity really is better. None of the stuff really matters, and you really can get along with a whole lot less. Stuff tends to accumulate and clutter not only homes but also hearts. Stuff isn't important after all. It can be replaced; people can't!

I have to say that, interestingly enough, not a single survivor I have worked with would choose to be the person they were pre-flood. They would perhaps not have addressed the important life issues that kept them "stuck." To say they would choose a disaster to happen to change them would be ludicrous, but they are thankful for the by-products; i.e., addressing important life issues that kept them stuck and unhealthy such as eliminating, reprioritizing, etc.

LET'S TALK SHOP

Let's look at some basics of trauma recovery. The media may recover quickly from a natural disaster, but people don't. For the media, the trauma, in this case the Tennessee Flood, was a story, an impersonal event in time. For victims of this or any other trauma, the trauma is not merely A story; it is THEIR story. It is not an impersonal event in time; it is a very personal event in time, which changes every other event in time in a very personal way.

The good news is people do generally recover from trauma, but like most everything, it takes time. It is a process, a painful, gradual process. It is often stressful, it involves grieving loss, and it requires the acceptance of change. It is also distinctly unique to each individual. While it's true that time is perhaps the best healer, the benefit of having someone to talk with honestly and openly about thoughts and feelings is immeasurable. That someone can be a friend or family member most certainly, but sometimes a skilled therapist or pastor can provide considerable benefit. People in the mental health profession are trained to help others process information, gain perspective, and provide a safe place to grow, adjust, and adapt.

For those of you reading this book who were survivors of the 2010 Tennessee Thousand-Year Flood or some other natural disaster, sometime, somewhere, chances are you have heard some of what follows. Let this be a refresher course. For those of you who weren't involved or haven't experienced a natural disaster or other trauma, thank God. For you, this can be a means of gaining understanding and empathy, and heaven forbid, gathering information for future reference.

THE THREE R'S OF RECOVERY

Experts in the field of recovery have identified three key components in the healing process: resistance, resiliency, and resources.

Resistance refers to the amount of "emotional stamina" an individual has to "weather the storm" of a trauma (no pun intended). The term is used frequently when speaking of physical recovery. When a person is physically healthy; i.e., eats right, exercises, and has an uncompromised immune system, that person can resist or heal quickly from illness. When people are not healthy, resistance is low and the chance of contracting a disease is high. Conversely, the possibility of making a quick recovery, or even recovering at all, is unlikely.

The same is true of emotional health. When a person is healthy emotionally; that is, manages stress, has a positive attitude, has set goals and is routinely meeting them, has an adequate support system, etc., that person can resist or fight back emotional illness (i.e. depression, anxiety, etc.). When he or she is unhealthy, resistance is low and the chance of contracting an "emotional disease" is high, and the chance of recovering quickly or ever is low.

The Three R's of Recovery – Pam

Resiliency refers to "bounce back." It speaks to how quickly a person can restore himself or herself to a previous level of functioning. Experts don't know much about what makes one person more resilient than another. Studies on resiliency have been conducted with abused children, and time after time, the findings are the same. One child struggles with post-trauma while his sibling functions well. It is believed that genetics play a role in resiliency. Parents and caretakers are also important. They model resiliency for children by responding positively to life's stresses and challenges.

Whether resiliency is more nature or nurture remains uncertain. It does, however; appear to be a combination of both, as well as personality type and character predisposition. I see this over and over in the therapy room. Siblings come in. Both have been victims of severe trauma and/or abuse. One is functioning very poorly, and the other is thriving. One is devastated while the other can scarcely recall details and is well adjusted. Of course, resiliency is clearly impacted by the duration and severity of the trauma. Also important to consider is quantity. Simply stated, our resiliency weakens if there is little to no recovery period between traumatic events.

Resources refer to what we have at our disposal to help support recovery—that which helps us get things done and figure things out. We have the most control in this area. If family and friends are not viable, positive resources, we must find help elsewhere. Therapeutic help abounds, and support groups are prevalent. Of course, we can also teach ourselves new skills by reading books, researching online, asking questions, and taking a class or workshop. The point is that when we are informed or know where to get informed, when we know how to help ourselves or know where to go for help, we are better able to recover more quickly and fully.

UNDRESSING STRESS – WHAT IS IT? WHAT DOES IT DO?

At this point, it's important to address the issue of stress and the role it plays in recovery from trauma. Let's start undressing stress by looking at a few different definitions. A good place to start is with Webster, which defines stress as "pressure, strain, or force that produces change." That's pretty generic. It could be referring to heavy machinery or the human machine.

The Mayo Clinic describes stress as "normal psychological and physical reaction to the demands of life." The brain perceives a threat, and the body releases hormones to fuel a fight, flight, or freeze response. When the threat is gone, the body returns to normal. Because modern life presents virtually non-stop stress, the alarm system rarely shuts off. Stress management, therefore, is something we must learn to do in order to maintain mental, emotional, and physical health. We are talking about the constant need to address one change after another after another.

Psychologists define stress as "exposure to events that threaten our environment, thwart expectations, intimidate our resources, and require change." According to the Critical Incident Stress Management Foundation, an organization which assists globally in disaster relief and trauma response on a mass scale, stress is a "response to stimulus (change) and is characterized by physical and psychological arousal."

According to all four definitions, change is the name of the game, and we don't like it, do we? The good news about change is that we can control about 75 percent of anything that can happen to us. The trick is to know what I can control and what I cannot. In the case of a natural disaster, of course, we have no control over its occurrence, only over our response to it.

All change, even good change, is stressful. When we are stressed, our energy and stamina levels are reduced, and our physical, cognitive, emotional, and psychological resources are challenged. Our resistance and resiliency are both compromised. As a result, our behavior looks different. Things we normally handle with ease and efficiency become chores. Information we generally process quite handily becomes overwhelming and confusing. Think of us as that human machine I referred to earlier. Change causes stress, and stress causes our systems to become overloaded or over-stimulated. Instead of overheating or blowing a circuit, as is the case with a machine, humans go into a conservation mode in order to reserve energy. Much like a machine, we, too, convert from manual to automatic.

Another way to look at this is with a nutrition metaphor. When we restrict caloric intake and eat too little, our bodies go into starvation mode. They prepare for the need to "stretch" those calories over a longer period of time and slow down the system in preparation for survival. The same is true with emotional overload. The mind prepares to stretch limited energy resources over a longer period of time. Because our system cannot shut down and reboot like a computer can, it simply slows down to regroup, redirect, and recharge.

There are some common behavioral, emotional, physical, and mental reactions to stress. Some are outwardly apparent, others not as visible. The following checklist is taken from the Individual Crisis Counseling Services Encounter Log used by FEMA:

Behavioral
- Extreme change in activity level
- Excessive drug or alcohol use
- Isolation/withdrawal
- On guard/hypervigilant
- Agitated/jittery/shaky
- Violent or dangerous behavior
- Acts younger than age (children or youth)

Emotional
- Sadness, tearful
- Irritable, angry
- Anxious, fearful
- Despair, hopeless
- Feelings of guilt/shame
- Numb, disconnected

Physical
- Headaches
- Stomach problems
- Difficulty falling or staying asleep
- Eating problems
- Worsening of health problem
- Fatigue, exhaustion

Mental
- Distressing dreams, nightmares
- Intrusive thoughts, images
- Difficulty concentrating
- Difficulty remembering things
- Difficulty making decisions
- Preoccupied with death/destruction.

ADDRESSING STRESS

We've undressed stress to examine what's underneath it. Now let's address it. We've talked about the fact that some changes in life are beyond our control. However, there are many things in life that we can control. To manage stress effectively, it's important to know what stresses us out. It's also important to keep track of our stress level at any given point in time. This may take a little work at first, and you may want to seek the help of a close friend, a family member, or a counselor as you begin a self-evaluation. I personally have gotten help from all three sources and not just once or twice, but many, many times. The truth is we need one another to get through life, even on an average, run-of-the-mill day, and all the more on days when stress runs high.

OK, now, not to go all therapist on you, but I do want you to have some information that I've come across over the years and have found useful. Remember information is power, and awareness is information. In the case of stress, what you don't know could well hurt you. So, become more self-aware. Head on back to the appendix to the stress surveys and assessments provided and get to know yourself!

You could wait and do it on a rainy day. Better yet, do it sooner, just in case the rainy day goes all crazy on ya!

Here's what you'll find in the appendix:

1. **Holmes & Rahe Stress Scale** – Stress level indicator based upon number of changes/transitions within a one-year period.
2. **Personality Type Stress Susceptibility Test** – Identifies personality type and associated susceptibility to stress reaction.
3. **Success with Stress Test** – Measures resiliency to stress based on healthy lifestyle habits.
4. **100 Stress Busters.**

Change your thoughts! It's for your own good!

Listen! There's no way around it. What we think matters. We are what we think we are. Others are what we think they are. The world is what we think it is. It's all very subjective. Here's how the whole thinking thing works: What we think determines what we believe, which impacts how we feel, which leads to our actions, and every action has a reaction or consequence. When we change our thoughts, we change our lives, or at least the way we see them or perceive them.

The first order of business is looking at our worldview. I had the privilege of a wonderful 10-year friendship with Phyllis Eliot, widow of the late Dr. Robert S. Eliot, cardiologist, past director of the Institute of Stress Medicine in Denver, Colorado, and author of the book *From Stress to Strength*. Dr. "Bob" found there to be two basic worldview groups of people. Group 1 is the FUD group. These are the people who see the world as filled with fear, uncertainty, and doubt—FUD. Then, there is the NICE group. These are the people who see the world as filled with newness, interest, creativity, and excitement. In his many years of practice, Dr. Eliot found that NICE people consistently lived longer and healthier than FUD-dyduds (I made that up) and he encouraged FUDDERS (he made that up) to change their worldview for their own good. Remember how your mom always told you to be nice? Who knew it would be good for your health as well as your social life?

As a cognitive behavioral therapist, I couldn't agree more. I spend many hours every week helping others change distorted ways of thinking into healthy ways, change the internal monologue called self-talk from negative to positive. The late Dr. Albert Ellis, founder of Rational Emotive Behavior Therapy, called negative self-talk and cognitions "stinking thinking." He was right. They stink up a person's life and permeate into everyone else's life who might be close enough to "catch a whiff." Do you need to clean up your act? Are you the skunk in the room? Just like the elephant in the room that won't go away until it is addressed, the stench has to be dealt with. And only you can do it! I know. I've cleared out a number of rooms in my day.

The second area is that of connectedness. Experts in the mental health field have long identified three key factors in determining a person's ability to manage change and challenge, in short, life. They are: a) a positive and fulfilling intimate relationship, b) a strong support network of friends, and c) a spiritual belief system. How do you look in these three areas? If not good, do something about it. Find people you can connect with. Find a higher power you can believe and have faith in.

The last area I will refer to as PMS. That's right, PMS. No! Premenstrual Syndrome is not on the stress management list, this is a different PMS, the one we actually need all month long, every month. PMS refers to purpose, meaning, and service. In measuring overall mental health, professionals know that without a purpose, without meaning, and without the ability to give by serving, we are at risk of developing mental health issues. Ask yourself these questions: "Do I have someone or something to love, something to learn, something to do, someone to help?" Well, do you? If you don't, get that handled! Figure it out!

All of the above play an important role in determining an individual's unique outcome when stress and trauma strike. By outcome, I mean recovery; how long will it take, and what it will look like.

COME ON! LIGHTEN UP A LITTLE!

Those of us with kids are quite familiar with the question, "Whatcha got in your backpack?" Usually the question is asked when attempting to remove that no-kindergartener-should-be-carrying-something-this-heavy thing off the six-year-old's shoulders.

The answer is typically, "Nothing, Mom."

But, that's not the case. Once it's opened, it's obvious that it hasn't been cleaned for only God knows how long. What looks like a science experiment gone bad is just a three-month-old PB & J sandwich.

Many of us carry around a much too heavy backpack as well. All too often, we have acquired things and placed them in our "life backpack," things we just don't need anymore, perhaps never needed. Much will have outlived its usefulness, like the torn, wrinkled first-day-of-school assignment we find during spring break. I should know. I AM the queen of hanging on to stuff I don't need to any longer. As Emily Barnes, author of *More Hours in My Day*, a book on organization, says, "Put it away, throw it away, or give it away."

We all need to look inside the invisible backpacks we carry filled with our unique set of "stuff" regularly and see what needs to be removed. You might say, "But I don't carry around anything unnecessary in my life backpack. I've dealt with my issues. I've gotten rid of the extra weight." OK, fine. So you might be one of the perfect ones. This is for the rest of us, then, the imperfect ones.

Here's the thing. Sometimes we just don't have that much control over what gets put in there. Also remember that people and situations are constantly changing the contents, and we are constantly adjusting and adapting in response. Do yourself a favor! Take a look inside, and lighten up! And do it regularly!

Here are some of the common things we tend to carry around that weigh us down. I personally can check off almost all of them.

- The need to control
- Conflict in our close relationship(s)
- Unforgiveness
- Unresolved grief
- Lack of assertiveness
- Anger
- Financial pressure/excessive debt
- Over commitment
- Confused or non-existent spiritual belief system
- Indecision
- Clutter
- Perfectionism
- Isolationism
- Unhealthy friendships
- Drug and alcohol abuse/dependency

- Unhealthy diet
- Lack of exercise
- Job dissatisfaction

HOW MANY A'S IN ANTI-STRESS? EIGHT!

The key to managing stress is staying on top of it and taking charge of it. Here are eight ways to change distress to de-stress. I call them the Eight As. We've already talked about them, but to recap, here they are:

1. **Awareness** – Become and stay aware of the sources of stress in your life. Plato said, "The unexamined life is the wasted life."
2. **Activate a plan** – Take control of your calendar and your life. Learn to say no; recognize the "warning signs" of stress. OK, I am definitely preaching to the choir on this one. Ask yourself this question! Do you always start to get sick when you have too much going on? Listen to that sore throat, that achy body, that headache! "There is a fallow time for the spirit when the soil is barren because of sheer exhaustion" (Howard Thurman).
3. **Avoid unnecessary stress** – Take control of your environment—avoid people, places, and things that

stress you out whenever possible. I know what you're about to say. How can I avoid my husband? The dentist's office? That gossipy group at church? I said whenever possible, didn't I?!
4. **Alter the situation** – Figure out what you can do to change things, be as assertive as possible, and be willing to compromise.
5. **Adapt to the stressor** – If you can't change the stressor, work to change your expectations and attitude. Pastor Chuck Swindoll, long-time pastor of one of the largest Evangelical Free Churches in America and author of countless books, writes, "I am convinced that life is 10% what happens to me and 90% how I react to it. And so it is with you… you are in charge of your attitude."
6. **Accept the things you can't change** – Some stressors are unavoidable, i.e., death, many illnesses, the state of the economy, lack of world peace, terrorism, natural disasters, etc. No words speak to this more eloquently than the often-quoted "Serenity Prayer" by Reinhold Niebuhr: "God grant me the serenity to accept the things I cannot change; courage to change the things I can; and wisdom to know the difference."
7. **Allocate time for R&R** – Have fun, laugh, and play. This is not a luxury; it's a necessity. We would all do well to follow the advice of poet Robert Frost, "To find yourself you must be lost enough." Set aside time to do nothing. Also set aside time to do something, something you enjoy or something that feeds your soul, or better yet, both. You know what makes you feel reenergized. Go do it!
8. **Adopt a healthy lifestyle** – Take care of your whole self. Remember, we spoke of the close interconnectedness among mind, body, soul, and spirit? You know the drill here. You know it, but

do you do it? Do you exercise, eat a healthy diet, limit caffeine and alcohol, avoid cigarettes and drugs, get enough sleep, visit your health care practitioner regularly?

We've included in the appendix 100 STRESS BUSTERS to get you started on the journey toward "stess-less" living. Why not try one a day for the next 100 days. Who knows? You just might change your life in those three months.

You can also find these ready to print on our website (www.waves-of-change.net).

PART V

HOPE SPRINGS ETERNAL

HOPE, RESILIENCY, AND COURAGE

Hope, resiliency, and courage are essential for life. They are also critical for recovery from crisis, loss, and disaster. If we are to recover, we need hope that there will be better moments ahead of us, resiliency to endure what we are experiencing currently, and courage to maintain both of these. Only then can we keep moving forward successfully in an uncertain, sometimes painful world.

When I think back over the 2010 floods in Tennessee, these three words capture the response of those involved. Do you want to hear stories of hope, resiliency, and courage? Just listen to the 'voices' of brave men and women of fire departments, emergency medical personnel, police and sheriff departments, and emergency management offices! Day and night, on streets and in buildings, in boats and on foot, these people worked tirelessly to save those trapped by threatening floodwaters. Battling fatigue and discouragement, they searched for the bodies of those too late to save in order to return them to their loved ones and a dry resting place. When I think of those three words, I marvel at the countless Volunteer-State civilians who rose up higher than the rising waters all across Tennessee to do their part in the recovery effort during this unprecedented event in our history.

Reflecting on these three words, I see, too, the faces of thousands of flood survivors. Devastated by the loss of their homes, pets, priceless possessions, family members, far too many were subjected to secondary losses. Criminal contractors swindled many out of insurance money and disappeared leaving rebuilding projects unfinished. Still, survivors kept on working to rebuild.

Many were forced to forfeit hard-earned, lifelong savings and retirement money prudently set aside for financial security during their golden years. Disheartened, broke, and broken, they kept on working to rebuild. It took these valiant survivors an extra measure of hope, resiliency, and courage to move forward believing each new day would bring them closer to the normalcy and security they once knew. The thing is, rebuilt homes and restored bank accounts are one thing, hearts take much longer to rebuild and restore.

I also see hope, resiliency, and courage personified in the faces of those who lost a family member or friend during the flood or who lost a part of themselves—physically or emotionally—as a result of the flood. These courageous souls exemplify living with grace and hope in an often-harsh world. They teach us that it is possible to overcome terrible obstacles and painful losses.

As you, the reader, move forward from a crisis in your life, whether from natural disaster, or any other kind of loss, it is our profound desire that this book can help in some small way. There are no precise blueprints or personalized checklists on recovery. Every person is unique. We all draw on previous experiences, and chances are what has helped us in the past, will again be beneficial. We also all learn from others, benefitting from not only our own experiences, but also taking the lessons learned from others and applying them to our own challenging situations. That's the way it's been done since time immemorial—people helping people and neighbors helping neighbors, and it's even easier today to reach out and find support groups on the Internet. If you don't like the first group of like-minded individuals, you can always find another one.

We must also understand that disaster recovery is a practice at best—it's an art, not a science. Three years after the flood, we still have people trying to recover physically and/or emotionally. I can attest to this and so can Pam. Some survivors are still living in conditions in which not even a feral animal should live. As much as we all want to wave some kind of magic wand and restore everyone to the way they were before the disaster (or better yet help them be even better than they were before the disaster), that is an extremely difficult task. Actually, it's beyond difficult; it is in most cases, impossible. When loss happens, the world as you knew it is gone. In the case of a life being lost, that person is never going to come back; your world will never again have them in it. Thus, your world is forever changed.

Similarly, when a natural disaster happens, that home, that stuff, those things are never going to come back, your world will never again have them in it. You may have a rebuilt house, but not the one where you opened Christmas presents and drank hot cocoa, played Monopoly and card games, celebrated birthday parties, or splattered pancake batter on Saturday mornings. Your new home will not have laughter in the walls... yet. Likewise, you may get new appliances, but not the dishwasher that makes that squeaky sound that used to make you crazy, not the washing machine that always gets stuck on the spin cycle. These were like friends, too, and you miss them, annoying as they were.

You may have people like disaster relief workers and grief counselors help you recover, and recover you will. Things will return at some point to normal and become familiar, but it will be a new normal, an unfamiliar familiar.

The fact of the matter is, as others are busy building you a new home and bringing in new built-ins, you are even busier building you a new life. It's easy to forget weeks, months, years after a disaster that many survivors are still working hard to rebuild their lives. Just because the big organizations have wrapped up operations, and the media cameras have moved on to the "next big story," doesn't mean everyone has settled into to new normal status. This may be the perfect opportunity for you to organize your local church, neighborhood group, co-workers, or friends and find someone who hasn't yet found that new normal. Go ahead! Why not take the time to find them, go out of your comfort zone, and be inconvenienced. Wouldn't you want someone to find you and risk the discomfort and inconvenience if you were the one needing help finding your way 'back home'?

In every disaster, communities are faced with circumstances they have never faced before. Mistakes unfortunately happen but so do great acts of compassion and sacrifice. As long as everyone is striving to help their communities and the people in them rebuild and recover, it's possible, and necessary, to see past the mistakes and focus on everything that is going right. After all, we are all just flawed human beings.

As flawed humans, one thing that is important to remember and that will mitigate mistakes is the practice of good self-care. Remember that you need to take care of yourself no matter what your role is in a disaster—rescuer, survivor, recovery worker, grief counselor, or volunteer. Because no long-term time-outs are granted in life, just "mini time-outs," we need to take them when we can, and on a regular basis.

We all need to incorporate into our lives people, places, and things that make us feel good and keep our 'hope, resiliency, and courage tanks' full.' Running on an empty tank won't get you far in your automobile, nor will it get you far in life. Keep some reserve in your personal tank so you will be ready to play your role should a life crisis come your way. We seldom know when that day will come, and sometimes, life has an uncanny, unfortunate way of throwing one at us while we are still in the process of recovering from another one.

In closing, I would like to leave you with the "Story of the Starfish." A man was walking along the beach, and thousands and thousands of starfish had been washed up on the shore. He began to pick them up, one at a time, and toss them back into the sea. Another person came up and said, "What are you doing? Are you crazy? You cannot save all of these starfish. You are wasting your time and getting dirty for no reason."

The man looked up, tossed a starfish back into the sea and said, "Yes, but I made a difference for this one."

I have made this my personal motto in disaster relief work. Because a situation can look so bleak, overwhelming, and ominous when disaster strikes, I make it a point to focus on each person I meet and help that single starfish. I also keep in mind that no one person is capable of single-handedly saving everyone after a flood, tornado, tsunami, earthquake, fire, or any other unexpected threat, but I can make a tremendous difference one person at a time. I can make a worthy contribution that will have a lasting effect on others as long as I remember each starfish makes a difference, each one is important, each one deserves my effort, my attention, my very best.

It is our hope that the lessons we have learned and collected here can in some way ease your suffering should you and/or a loved one come face to face with a disaster. In sharing what we three have learned about hope, resiliency, and courage, it is our sincerest desire that others can build upon this—and that we can all work together in our respective communities to be survivors in the face of whatever disaster or crisis we may experience in the future.

WHEN THE STUDENT IS READY...
THE TEACHER WILL APPEAR

It's difficult to put a life-changing event into perspective until you've come out the other side. The process of surviving a disaster, rebuilding, and recovering is different for each person, so my experiences may not resemble yours.

We do share similarities when faced with a climactic event, however, such as the feeling of hitting rock bottom and having no idea how we will recover. When that happens, we're forced to start over. There's no other choice, and most of us rise to the occasion. It's how we get beyond the storm that differs for each of us. In the end, we come out a changed person, often a better person. It's almost impossible to come through a trauma without gaining greater understanding and empathy. We are the sum total of our experiences, and getting beyond a disaster is a major, life-changing experience that fundamentally changes who we are. In the process, we learn that life is a moving target.

My condo may never fully recover in terms of furnishings, and it certainly won't recover in terms of

When the Student Is Ready...
The Teacher Will Appear – MJ

irreplaceable items—that's why they're called irreplaceable—but I am so over this flood! It's a memory, one crisis in a succession of calamities that make up that thing we call life—no more, no less. It hasn't even earned the "worst thing that's ever happened to me" award. That's the upside for a person like me, a chaos magnet. The calamities just keep on flowing, with each one topping the previous one only **in that moment in time**. It's after the fact, when we have time to reflect, that we can put those moments into perspective.

Whenever I've been in the midst of chaos, it's been difficult to see the end of the rainbow. I know from experience that things do get better—they always do. It's part of the ebb and flow of life. The difficult part is remembering this when my comfortable life has suddenly exploded into tiny fragments.

It's even worse when the disasters come in rapid succession. I know, because I was there. Lucky for me, I've had a lot of practice at this. My TWA training taught me to get through an initial shock and fall apart later. My high-school years at St. Cecilia Academy taught me to bite my lip when necessary. My mother raised me to "just get over it." All of these experiences prepared me to deal with the flood. Other flood survivors used their life experiences to help them cope in different ways.

Of all the many lessons learned and/or applied, a handful will have the greatest effect on my life. These are my lessons, many of which I had to relearn because the student wasn't ready in the past. I hope that you can draw from some of them and apply them in your own life.

Think for yourself

When the authorities tell you to evacuate, you should have a very good reason for going against the grain, but if you do need to evacuate, you want to beat the crowd out of the area. You may have to travel back roads, so buy a local map, highlight alternate escape routes, and put it in your glove compartment—just in case. It couldn't hurt to drive a dry run on one or two of those routes some spring day when you're suffering from cabin fever.

My personal lesson learned is not to wait for the authorities to tell me to get out. I knew I needed to leave. I had empirical data—the nonstop torrents of pounding rain against my roof for two days—and I had a gut feeling. I chose to go against all that information. That was a mistake. It cost the life of my pet, and it could have cost mine as well. Had I taken the threat seriously, I would have moved irreplaceable items to the second story on Saturday night. I have an incredible sixth sense that visits me infrequently, and I usually heed its call. I don't get a do-over, but I do get to go forward with this knowledge indelibly etched on my brain.

I have thought back many times to 9/11 when the North Tower came crashing down. The occupants in the South Tower were ordered back into their offices. I remember my mother asking if I would have followed that order.

I looked at her as if she were crazy and said, "You know I wouldn't—not on your life. What is wrong with these people that they can't think for themselves?" And this exchange took place before the South Tower came down. I would never take an order seriously that would endanger my life; I don't care who issued it, and I never would have re-entered that tower—not even to grab my purse!

I once kept a full 747 bound for London the night before Thanksgiving from taking off for five hours. I accidentally found out that a specific threat had been made against our aircraft. When I went to the cockpit to inquire about this, I was told they didn't want a delay to "interfere" with our three-day layover.

When the Student Is Ready…
The Teacher Will Appear – MJ

I was furious that the captain (and it was the captain, not the rest of the pilots) would risk lives for a layover, and I made sure the rest of the cabin crew was sufficiently furious to have the passengers and baggage unloaded, rechecked, and every square inch of that aircraft inspected before we departed. I made a decision to risk my job over risking my life based on the information the Port Authority police slipped to me. I made a few well-placed calls from the jetway, and no one knew anything until the order was given to deplane. Who's to say that something wasn't planned in the air at a specific time and location and that we hadn't foiled the plan by altering our departure time? Oh, and as a bonus, I was never discovered as the culprit of the delay.

So what on earth was I thinking staying put against my better judgment and my gut feeling during the rain? First, I think I was out of practice. During the TWA years, I was in a perpetual state of heightened awareness, and while it had faded, it has returned since the flood. At the time, I put my faith in what everyone else was saying, "We haven't flooded in a hundred years, and we're not going to flood this time." I knew better, but I didn't act on what I knew because I didn't want to believe it would happen. I didn't think for myself, and look where it got me. You can benefit from my admission of failure if you think for yourself and trust your instinct.

Don't believe everything you hear
You will probably have warm and caring interactions with authorities and volunteers after a disaster. However, if you should run into an interaction like the one I had with the "mental health worker," take it with a grain of salt. It's one person's opinion, and the person could be just as stressed as you are. These people work around the clock in the immediate aftermath of a disaster, and they are probably on

their last raw nerve a few days into their shifts, with no end in sight.

Moreover, I wish those who volunteer in any capacity would incorporate the concept "do no harm." Disaster survivors have already had enough trauma inflicted upon them without it being piled on from volunteers with the best of intentions who are totally out of their element and in way over their heads. And to all the well-meaning agencies, I would suggest the following: The aftermath of a disaster is the **worst** possible time to institute the Peter Principle.

You can never be too prepared

It didn't take long for me to realize that you can never be too prepared for an emergency, and more importantly, that no two emergencies are alike. I thought that being able to handle a vast array of in-flight emergencies prepared me for anything in life I would ever face. I should have learned that lesson in the Gulf during the war, but it took the flood to drive the point home. How could I not be prepared for any in-flight emergency? I had practiced those procedures ad infinitum for a quarter of a century.

At TWA, we had a practice called the 30-second review. Before every take-off and landing, we were supposed to spend 30 seconds reviewing emergency evacuation procedures while buckled into our jump seats. I took little of the training seriously; I had my own way of doing things, but when it came to safety, I listened, learned, and carried through on the procedures. I always, without fail, performed the 30-second review.

I also knew the basic drill for a tornado, something completely random and out of our control. Floods, however, were not part of my disaster repertoire. They were nowhere to be found in my knowledge base other than the annual aircraft ditching simulations we rehearsed on dry land. Those simulations were no match for a flood or even a live ditching.

Floods and hurricanes are different from tornadoes and other sudden emergencies, and they give us an advantage over Mother Nature. They are not without warning, and we should have ample time to remove ourselves, our family, our pets, vital records, and backups of important computer data from harm's way. It's better to have backups off-site, but I would not consider saving anything to the cloud without thoroughly examining the terms of service (TOS). It's important to repeat that some of the cloud sites "own" anything uploaded to them (including proprietary client data), and that's not for me. That's where my trusted Passport drive came in handy.

Now that I've suffered the effects of a weather event and have learned the hard way that not all disasters are created equally, I have taken a page from the pilot playbook and formulated a plan and a checklist for each type of likely event. There's a reason that pilots have checklists. They need to go through a series of steps without stopping to think. The checklist does the thinking for them. The thought was put into developing the checklist; the checklist just ensures that no stone is left unturned each and every takeoff, landing, and anticipated emergency. We can take that lesson to heart and create our own checklists, rehearse in our minds our action plans until they become second nature. We can follow the checklist if and when the time comes.

It's amazing how you can apply prior experience if you take the time to find the parallels, make a few modifications, and then put together an action plan.

Some rainy day, when you have nothing better to do, make a list of important phone numbers and place it your wallet. It's a backup for your cell phone contacts list in case you lose access to your cell phone. You're unlikely to dash out, even in an emergency, without your wallet. Those phone numbers will come in handy once you've escaped a life-threatening situation.

Even with all my life experiences, I was woefully unprepared. Now that the flood is behind me, I have incorporated some of these procedures into my daily life. When the weather forecast even hints at the possibility of a weather event, I conduct a 30-second review before I go to sleep in case the event materializes. Usually, I just stay up all night because I'm part of an ad-hoc phone tree with friends in my county and an adjacent county.

While I don't pretend to know why, I do know weather trends and patterns (called climate) are changing. Weather events are coming in increasingly rapid succession, and they are more severe than in the past. We can carry on blissfully ignoring the obvious, or we can prepare ourselves. It looks like wherever you live, it's a matter of when, not if, some bizarre weather pattern will hit. You owe it to yourself, your family, and your pets to be prepared. It costs nothing to make a plan, rehearse it, and tweak it until you're comfortable that you can execute it on a moment's notice.

Step out of your comfort zone

I heard a man speak at a meeting held in Bellevue the week after the flood. He was discussing casualty losses, and much of what he said eluded me. Words, not numbers, are my medium of exchange, and I'm downright inadequate in the numbers department. I was lost after the first few sentences, but I found his casual and sometimes flip style engaging, even when I didn't understand a word he was saying.

Back in my room at the Microtel, I toyed with the idea of tracking him down and calling him, but cold calling is not something I'm comfortable doing. I couldn't find an email address, but I did find his phone number, and I was surprised to learn that he lived in an adjacent section of

When the Student Is Ready...
The Teacher Will Appear – MJ

River Plantation. I wondered and worried about the etiquette of calling him and asking him to share his expertise in a manner that I could understand. Finally, I dialed his number. He was incredibly helpful and didn't seem to mind the intrusion.

He and his wife have been friends since that very day and have introduced me to other wonderful neighbors in their section of River Plantation. I would not have the pleasure of knowing them if I hadn't stepped out of my comfort zone, and that is worth far more than the knowledge I gained from quizzing him on casualty losses.

Grief cannot be denied

I didn't learn this lesson fully until 2012. We can postpone grief, but we cannot deny it. It eventually catches up with us. The events of late 2008–2010 caught up with me on the morning of July 30, 2012.

The day started like any normal day. I was making coffee at 0-dark hundred, and the cats were chasing each other around the living room. I could hear the din in the kitchen, and I didn't think anything of it until the howls from Zorba grew louder and took on a desperate note. I went to see what Georgie was doing to annoy him, and to my horror, Zorba was panting and foaming at the mouth. I called my vet on his cell phone and told him to get here STAT and that cost was no consideration (even though, of course, it was).

Within 20 minutes, and long before the vet arrived, Zorba the Cat was dead. Having lost most of my cats to feline renal failure late in their teens and early in their twenties, I knew this was an unusual death. The vet explained it was some sort of spontaneous tipping of the stomach or twisted intestines. It didn't matter which. What mattered was that my precious Zorba was gone—a two-

and-a-half year old, seemingly healthy cat just dropped dead with no warning.

Zorba, you'll recall, was born the day of the flood, the day Miss Fluff died, and he was given to me the day I moved home. That furry little creature got me through the transition of moving back into surroundings that were foreign to me, and I know he was sent to me for that purpose. I have no doubt about that, but why did he have to go so early in his life? He was one of those rare "happy" cats, and he was Georgie's "best friend." And then—poof—just like he came into my life, he departed. Maybe, just maybe, he has found Miss Fluff, somewhere over the Rainbow Bridge.

Once the tears started flowing, they flowed for six straight weeks—and not just for Zorba. My parents' deaths, and the unfairness (randomness, to be more precise) of the flood had caught up with me. Zorba's death was just the latest icing on the cake. All these thoughts raced through my mind sending me into a meltdown. How could one person lose so much in so short a time? It just wasn't fair. (Life is not fair…blah, blah, blah…rinse, lather, and repeat as often as necessary…)

The next week, I found a book Kathy had given me a few years before tucked away in a bookcase upstairs. As I read *Animals as Teachers and Healers* from cover to cover over the weekend, the tears flowed in torrents, like the rain two years before. I couldn't stop crying. I cried for my parents and for everyone else who had ever died in my lifetime—friends, relatives, America as I used to know it, those I knew on TWA flight 800, and for those magical Christmases past that could never be again. I cried for all I had loved and lost. I cried about the flood—not about the actual flood, but about the flood being the last straw.

But wait, the flood wasn't the last straw—Zorba was. He was the straw that broke the camel's back and opened the floodgates of grief. Grief is painful, but delayed grief is a

When the Student Is Ready...
The Teacher Will Appear – MJ

bitch. (I don't recommend it.) In my case, there was little time to grieve until Zorba died because the events and challenges had kept coming in rapid succession, faster than I could grasp them.

Then one day six weeks later, I snapped out of it. I have no idea how it happened or what one thing caused the pain to ease. I still see the empty spots where Zorba lounged for hours on end. Georgie still mopes from time to time looking for Zorba, and I still look at his picture and tell him that I never would have made it through the transition home without him. He's not just some memory from the past; he's a comfort that I believe God and my mother sent to me in my time of need. And I have to believe he waited to move on until I was ready to stand on my own two feet.

Life is uncertain. Aside from death and taxes, the only guarantee in life is change; in my case, it was waves of change. But this event, no more than any other event, defines my life or my identity. It's just one in a series of events that has molded the person I call me. If there's one thing I can pass along to all disaster survivors, it is the wish that you don't allow a catastrophic event to overshadow all the good and all the wonder of life. Life is short; recovering from a disaster is but a small piece of the pie. In whatever way you can find to get on with your life, just get on with it and enjoy the high moments, savor them, and look back on them to carry you through your waves of change.

Appreciate what you have
Even in the midst of a catastrophe, we can find something to appreciate. We were living a surreal life after the flood. Each night, we found ourselves in relatively comfortable surroundings. But when the morning came, it was back to a war zone that slowly gave way to a *Sanford and Son* set as the weeks marched on. It was like living an episode of *The Twilight Zone* that would not end. Still, my neighbors and I

weren't living in our cars; we had clean places to rest our heads at night and loving friends and/or family to see us through this time.

In addition, we looked forward to our weekly coffee klatches. We appreciated the grants that came our way, the meals we were still able to eat, the fact that we were all in this together. There's always something to appreciate. Most of all, we could appreciate that we had survived, unlike so many other Tennesseans. And, when compared to other disaster survivors, we could appreciate that we were Tennesseans, specifically Nashvillians.

As time wore on, we realized that friends who came to our aid were real friends (like the friend and colleague who helped edit this book). They not only got involved but also stuck by us at our worst. Friends are to be treasured; unlike family, we get to choose friends, and when we choose wisely, they are there to shed light during our darkest hours.

Find and relish the humor

"Humor," you ask? Yes, there's humor all around us even in our bleakest moments. Every time I have hit rock bottom, humor has cushioned the fall. I didn't necessarily go looking for humor, but it always found its way to me—just like chaos and always on the heels of chaos. You may find fault in the examples that come next, and if you do, all I can say is, "Oh well! It works for me, but your mileage may vary." It's just one of a bag full of coping mechanisms. If you don't like this one, find one that works for you.

During a strike at TWA, I was out of work for three long years. One day, I was living the high-flying lifestyle, and the next day I was grounded, my wings clipped. When your entire identity is tied to "**what** you do" instead of "**who** you are" and it suddenly vanishes, so does a major part of you. (Incidentally, that was the biggest lesson I learned during the strike.)

When the Student Is Ready…
The Teacher Will Appear – MJ

The strike was devastating, even resulting in a few suicides, but as the strike wore (war) on, strikers found highly amusing ways to entertain ourselves. One Halloween, a group of us lit a bonfire and decided to burn our uniforms. The only problem (which we didn't know at the time) was that when we returned to work, we had to purchase new uniforms if we didn't have our old ones. I mustered up a tear, walked into a supervisor's office, and declared, "There was a fire." Those were the only words I could get out without laughing. No one asked any questions, and I got a free uniform **ensemble** (not just the basics) out of the deal. I laughed myself silly all the way down to the uniform office—even harder than when I had watched the first set go up in flames.

When my mother spent two weeks dying in Alive Hospice, my only sanity during that time was my cousin. Every night when I returned home, I would call her, and we would end up crying—not just over Mother's fate, but also from laughter over silly things, usually at the expense of one of the relatives who didn't like my mother. This is the only thing that gave me the courage to face the next day, another long day at Alive Hospice watching my mother wither away.

When my father died, just a year after Mom took her final breath, we held the visitation at the church. The priest knew that the sanctuary would fill to overflowing. The only thing he asked was that we kept it to a dull roar.

Like most "Southern gentlemen," my father loved Jack Daniels. As an airline management employee, he must have amassed 500 miniatures from the airplane over the years. (Management taking miniatures is promotion; flight attendants taking miniatures is stealing, so all the miniatures were his.) Every time he went to some function with an open bar, he filled his pockets with Jack Daniels and shared them with his friends.

Just as the crowd peaked at the visitation, one of his friends, a retired Jack Daniels executive, pulled out two Jack Daniels miniatures and said, "Boy, I'll bet Tommie could use one of these right about now."

I asked him if I could have one, and he gave it to me. As inconspicuously as possible, I tucked it into Dad's casket. I didn't know that the bottom of the casket was unlined, and at the exact moment that I dropped it into the casket, the crowd grew silent. The bottle dropped to the bottom, and the clang of the glass hitting metal in a dead-silent sanctuary with high ceilings and terrific acoustics was deafening.

Dad's friend and I burst out laughing; mine was no demure chuckle. All eyes turned toward the casket, Dad's friend, and me. We laughed even harder. We were out of control. If Dad had been there, he would laughed along with us. Relatives with no sense of humor rallied to the scene to see if I had taken total leave of my senses.

Were any of these responses "appropriate"? I doubt it, but I don't care. They got me through the moment without hurting myself or anyone else. Anyone whom I might have embarrassed was already dead or nowhere to be found. When I look back on these hard times, I always remember the lighter moments. It's not all gloom and doom.

I didn't realize the full value of humor until I interviewed a priest's wife for a magazine article. I was tasked with providing profiles of 12 remarkable women, all married to priests, who didn't necessarily follow the party line. It took a few weeks just to ferret out these exceptional women, but I was told specifically to include one woman. I had no idea why. She was a woman in her late 60s or early 70s, and she didn't possess any exceptional qualities that I could discern. I was told she was responsible for the sale of many subscriptions. Great—just great! This went against everything I stood for as a writer, but it was part of the assignment, and it was what it was, so I was determined to make it work.

When the Student Is Ready...
The Teacher Will Appear – MJ

About an hour into the interview, I had nothing fit to print. I was in a panic and ready to throw the keyboard across the room. Then, the dam burst, and it all became apparent to me. Aside from being a non-traditional priest's wife (no cooking for the church for this woman) and being less than thrilled that her husband had decided to join the clergy (all non-printable from my point of view), she was a cancer survivor and had survived two other life-threatening medical situations. Three times she had cheated death. When I started asking questions about how she had survived all of this, I didn't get what I expected. I expected some well-rehearsed drivel about faith and how God had pulled her through because he had greater plans for her—you know, the usual insipid reply that would put the readers to sleep.

Oh, no—I got nothing of the sort. She had turned to the Internet for humor. She told me that she didn't care what anyone thought. (That was obvious from her non-traditional attitude.) Instead, she had immersed herself in humor, and little by little, she fought off all of these life-threatening conditions. She attributed it to force-feeding herself humor and suggested that I look into this thing called YouTube. (Really? YouTube? LOL!) I took a chance and wove a story around all of her non-traditional attitudes, even the part about telling her husband "to go ahead and become a priest so you won't hate me for life."

When she saw the article, she called me. She told me that she had cried when she first read it, and for a split second, waves of terror raced through my veins. She went on to say she had cried tears of joy—that no one had ever given her such a heartfelt tribute because all the tributes had been saved for her husband.

They say humor is the best medicine, but to see it in action in such a dramatic form, where it saved a life, not once but three times, left an impression on me. It gave me permission to enjoy humor whenever and wherever it presents itself.

You will not be defined forever by a crisis

It's easy to forget that we are defined by the sum of our experiences when we go through a crisis. The designation "disaster survivor" does not define who we are. It simply defines our situation at a specific time.

A couple of months after the flood, one of my neighbors commented that there were only two types of people—those who flooded and those who didn't. Later, I thought back over my shared personal crises. I realized that for a short period after each of these crises, there were only two types of people—those who were affected by the crisis and those who were not, and it was difficult communicating with those who had not experienced the crisis firsthand. However, as time wore on, the divide always healed.

When I was referred to as a "survivor" in the third person (she's a flood survivor) as if it were my defining characteristic, it quickly grew old. And when others asked, "How **ARE** you," as if I were ready to crumble into a heap on the floor, I had to slip into "grace under pressure" mode. The combination of that tone of voice and the fact that the person asking obviously thought I was damaged goods was enough to send me into orbit by summer's end. I had to learn to exercise some sensitivity and empathy when others didn't realize that enough was enough. They meant well, and they were trying to help.

Often, our only previous point of comparison to a disaster is death, and no one knows exactly what to say when extending condolences. We need to take it easy on well-meaning family and friends. Sometimes they see us as victims rather than survivors. They may even refer to us as victims. I still take every opportunity to correct their terminology because words have meaning.

When the Student Is Ready…
The Teacher Will Appear – MJ

At some point, we may need to let them know gently **we have moved on**, we are not defined by our disaster, and we have rejoined life as their equal. If that doesn't work, we might have to move on without them. I found the people who kept referring to my survivor status as if it were a terminal illness are "glass half full" types, and it's best for me to run as fast as I can from them when I'm not at the top of my game.

LESSONS LEARNED

Did the 2010 Tennessee Flood teach me anything about life, others, or myself? Ah, yes indeed it did! About life it taught me first and foremost, that is, it reminded me to value, always value, each and every day. We simply never know what the next day will bring, or whether it will come at all for us.

Watch for hidden blessings in life

It also proved to me once again that often blessings come in surprising packages. I have had the privilege of meeting and working with 35 remarkable human beings whose paths most likely would not have crossed my own had it not been for the flood. I do not for one moment believe that our meeting was accidental, but rather I see each life I have been allowed a glimpse into, to have been a divine appointment. What I have learned from these survivors about the power and strength of the human spirit is immeasurable. I have witnessed firsthand the miraculous capacity of that spirit to heal and overcome.

Let go of the need to be in control

The vast majority of these 35 clients have reminded me of myself far more than I care to admit regarding the need to have power and control. You think I don't recognize the language, the demeanor of a control freak? I can spot one a mile away. I have spent most of my life being one. We want to control everything and everybody. We see control as power. We operate under the illusion that if we maintain the control, we will have enough power to protect ourselves from hurt, pain, and grief. We presume that it is possible to prevent the unanticipated and unplanned from entering into our "bubble of safety."

What is the cure for "control freakism"? The cure is the unexpected, the situation that limits our human strength, removes our resources, and blocks our abilities. For me it was the move to Tennessee, being uprooted from the known and familiar—no friends, little family, no church, no license to practice psychotherapy, no cultural understanding, not even a familiarity with the towns, streets, or the highways. For the flood survivors plagued with the "control" disease, it was the flood.

Oddly enough, almost everyone feels free when they finally come to the realization that they can't control every aspect of their lives, when they admit that they're powerless. Tom Hanks in the movie *Cast Away* encounters his freedom the moment he realizes he is never going to get off the island and is going to die completely alone. "The only choice I had—the only thing I could control—was when, how, and where that was going to happen... then a warm feeling came over me like a blanket when I realized that I had power over nothing."

The famous French philosopher Rene Descartes said, "I think therefore I am." God said, "I Am that I Am." Which sounds better to you? Does my ability to think, reason, and process really give me power and control? Over what? And, what happens when that ability diminishes or ceases? Do I fail to be an "I am" when I can no longer think clearly or logically, as is the case when trauma strikes? Do I fail to be an "I am" when I can no longer think at all, as is the case with those stricken with head injury or dementia?

Because God is constant, never changing, I can and should put my hope in Him. He is the One who can and does have the control and power. The good news is this Powerful Being loves me and promises to care for me. Giving my need to control over to Him is a wise choice, is the right choice if I want to find hope, peace, purpose, even when I lose all or most of what I have.

Of course, this brings us to the issue of faith. Over my 50+ years, both general observation in the 'room of life' and close scrutiny in the therapy room support the well-researched finding that those with faith fare better than those without it. Simply stated, those who are most resilient, resistant, and resourceful hold to a truth that there is a master plan. They believe in an intentional design by a sovereign, loving Creator who somehow is working all things together for an overall purpose, an aggregate good. These people recover quicker, and they adapt and adjust better to transition and change.

Those who contend that life is rather random, circumstantial, and accidental tend to recover more slowly or not at all, often remaining "stuck" in a victim mindset. For them, change brings anxiety, and they are constantly on "overload," unable to contemplate change. It's the difference between living in a state of need vs. living in a state of faith. It is the distinction between focusing on my circumstances (i.e., when they will change, how they are so unfair, etc.) vs. focusing on my relationship with my Creator. My clients who have given up trying to "conquer life," who have accepted their limitations, who trust and believe in a power greater, better, or smarter than their own have found their way to a healing place. If you have the choice between hopelessness, resignation, and remorse and purpose, peace, and satisfaction, isn't the latter the better choice?

It really is about resolving the conflict between despair and integrity. Erik Erikson, father of the Psychosocial Theory of Human Development, was right. He identified this conflict as the final struggle the ego would need to overcome. It involves looking at your life and feeling basically good about who you are and what you have done vs. feeling bad about a wasted, unproductive, and purposeless existence. Henry David Thoreau penned, "The mass of men live lives of quiet desperation." The Talmud, however; puts it this way, "Every blade of grass has its Angel that bends over it and whispers. Grow, grow."

Quite honestly, flood survivors and clients in general remain "stuck" in despair when, in pondering their lives, they conclude it "wasn't supposed to be like this… it didn't go according to plan." When it wasn't in their "script," wasn't part of the "vision," they struggle to find a place of acceptance. Gratitude eludes them, and hope and faith cannot be found. This to me is the saddest part of my job. I desperately want to "unstick" them, but you cannot take someone to a place they are not willing to go. Sometimes I lose these clients to suicide; they simply cannot find hope or cannot endure the pain of despair. This was the unfortunate case with one of my 35 clients.

Get used to change—it's a constant

Another thing the flood reinforced is the fact that change will come. I may not like it, I may not want it, but come it will. I don't like it any more than my clients do. The thing is, we don't have to like it necessarily, but we do have to accept it. In the case of the "my life wasn't supposed to look this way" clients, they will not heal until they accept that the life they are living IS, in fact, their life, the only one they get. They MUST change the way they think about it. As a cognitive behavioral therapist, I am constantly telling my clients to change their thoughts. It is the starting point for changing beliefs, feelings, actions, and consequences.

Many clients can't do it. They tell me so. What I tell them is, "Can't can mean won't or don't know how. If you mean 'won't,' I will not be able to help you through this struggle. If you mean 'don't know how,' I CAN help." I tell them exactly what I tell my kids when they say, "I don't want to do that." I say, "There are plenty of things I don't want to do either. Root canals, mammograms, and colonoscopies are at the top of the list, not to mention aging, and some days just plain ol' getting out of bed. Ya just gotta suck it up and do it." The same is true of accepting what is vs. what isn't! Ya just gotta do it!

I don't know why it is we get so attached to what is and so surprised and often distraught when what was, isn't anymore, or what is wasn't "what it was supposed to be." Let's get real! In my opinion, for what it's worth, most of my life "wasn't supposed to look THIS way." Are you kidding? Teenagers aren't supposed to have their moms die on them. Dads aren't supposed to be alcoholics. Divorces aren't supposed to break children's hearts. The adoptee who finally finds her birth mother is supposed to have a wonderful, Oprahesque reunion complete with warm, long-awaited invitations into the family she never knew. Surely I wasn't supposed to be 'sent away' after a lifetime-waited-for-dinner with nothing to hold on to but a "'don't call me, I'll call you, but at least you have some medical history now' farewell."

Here's the bottom line. We may not like how our story reads, but it's the only one we've got. Learning to accept what is vs. what isn't is a giant, grown-up step toward changing the state of our mental health.

Why is it so hard to change the way we look at things? I don't know. It just is. The funny thing is that the concept of change is something we are quite familiar with. We change our clothes, the oil in our car every so often (for me, to my husband's chagrin, not nearly often enough), and our home décor to match the coming holiday. Tide, time, and seasons all remind us that the world is in a constant state of change and transition—so does gravity (those body parts were much less saggy a few years ago) and natural selection (those animals looked different a few hundred years ago).

Take advantage of help when it's available

One thing I am certain we all need to change is the reluctance to ask for help when we need it. I know for me, I have starred far too many times in the "I'm isolating because life hurts" movie. When life gets overwhelming, or when I feel like no one can relate to "where I'm at," I 'go into hiding.' The very time when we most need help is when we least go find it. Flood survivors have told me everything from "I knew there were those far worse off than me who needed help much more than I did, and the resources should go to them," to "I was always more comfortable handling things on my own. I don't like asking for help. I've always been self-sufficient. I'm also very private. I'll manage—thanks, but no thanks."

To the first group, my question is, "How do you know?" To the second group my question is, "How's that working for you right about now?"

Can I be honest? This is just stupidity. When help is offered, take it! I used to be all about unloading the groceries into my car. Now when the box person asks if I want help out to my car, I say, "Yes, absolutely. My car's parked this way. Follow me." It was as though there was some type of imaginary reward awaiting me if, in fact, I could do it all. It's possible this is carry-over mentality from the '80's Superwoman Syndrome, which I found out the hard way was about a mythological character.

To the first ridiculous group of people I would say, "You're right, there may be somebody worse off than you; there may not be. The thing is, your loss is your loss, your struggle, your struggle. It all counts." To the second even more ridiculous group I would say, "That's fine. You can go back to handling things on your own when you're stable, but right now, you need help, and help is available. Let's get you some counseling to rebuild your life, and let's get some funding to rebuild your house... maybe even throw in a fridge or washer and dryer."

I've had clients tell me they were one of the last approved for funding assistance because they waited so long. They tell me how glad they are that they finally called. They realize they would never have been able to repair their home as quickly or nicely, and they would never have been able to afford the new appliances provided through grant money. Not to toot my own horn, but they may not have been able to afford the kind of quality counseling I provide either. Likewise, they may not have agreed to it had it not been paid for by flood recovery money because they prefer not to use financial resources for "frivolous" things like mental health. Or they may not have been able to get to a counselor due to physical or mental illness and/or lack of transportation. I was compensated for going to them, kind of like a doctor making house calls. Now there's a lost art!

This concept of the importance of accepting help when it is offered is perhaps best illustrated in this modern day parable told to me by a good friend. "One day a preacher found himself in peril. The floodwaters were rising all around him when a National Guard truck came by his house to save him. He refused the help asking them instead to save the many others who needed their help more. He told them, "The Lord will look after me." The water kept rising and the good preacher was forced to a second floor window where a group of rescuers came by in a boat to take him to safety. Again he refused, asking instead that they save others who needed their help. He said, "The Lord will look after me." The water kept rising and forced him to the roof of his house where finally a helicopter came to airlift him to safety. A third time he refused, saying he had faith the Lord would look after him. Finally, the preacher's house was completely engulfed in water, and he drowned. Upon arrival to heaven, wracked with disappointment and anger, he bitterly told St. Peter that he just couldn't believe the Lord had failed him. "Failed you…," St. Peter replied. "We sent you a truck, a boat, and a helicopter."

Final Thoughts
A few final thoughts—disaster, trauma, and loss are enemies of us all. They have no respect for individuals. I have seen flood clients who are wealthy and those who are poor, those who have dark skin and light skin, a doctoral level education and a learning disability, those who qualify for a student discount, and those who quality for a senior discount. These foes are the great equalizers.

The 2010 Tennessee Flood brought unexpected people with the same basic wants and needs into one another's lives, and I was one of them. Broken people. Different reasons, different sources. Broken all the same. I have a question for us all. Could it be that we are all better, stronger in some strange way because of the flood… because of the move… because of whatever it is that takes us down, but not out? I don't know for sure, but I think the answer is yes. Orthopedic specialists tell us that sometimes broken bones heal stronger and work better than before the break. I would like to think the same is true of hearts.

I never thought I would thank God for bringing me to Tennessee just in time for a flood of all things. But I do! As strange as that sounds, this unexpected, unwanted move afforded me the unique and unforgettable privilege of connecting with the hearts of 35 unexpected people. What an unspeakable blessing to have been a small part of the healing and recovery process for these amazing individuals for such a time as this. What's more, they were a part of my healing. We were on one another's 'heart stretcher squads'.

I helped carry them, and they, unknowingly, helped carry me.

I don't pretend to have a clear understanding of all the reasoning and purpose behind a natural disaster, or a cross-country move, or much of anything for that matter. I know for a fact that three years post-flood, many survivors continue to wrestle with life changes the flood brought. Just as I continue to wrestle with life changes the move to Tennessee brought about. When you have lost your home, either because of a flood or other natural disaster, or because you left it behind due to a move, a divorce, or a foreclosure, it's challenging to feel 'at home,' to find 'home.' What is home anyway? Is it where you hang your hat, where you go at the end of the long workday, or is it somewhere far more abstract?

Sometimes I feel like a Californian who makes her home now in Tennessee—sometimes a Tennessean who left her heart in some obscure corner of her California closet along with many memories, bent hangers, and dust balls—sometimes both and sometimes neither. It does seem to come in waves. I guess change is just that way! It comes in waves, and so does adjusting to it. I do know this. I am so much better than I was three years ago. Most days now, I'm just fine, and on the days I'm not fine, I remind myself that I will be fine again as I have so many times before.

MOVING FORWARD

People regain a semblance of normalcy at different paces. I say "semblance" because what comes after is a new normal. You may return to a nice, new home, but everything's different. Everything's new, and it's not as if you decided to redecorate. You had to make many decisions under duress if you wanted to get back home in a timely fashion.

I couldn't tell you when the transition started for me, but it happened in stages. I remember thinking, "Enough of this damn flood! I'm over it." That's how I deal with disappointment: I ache until I don't. When there's less return on investment in hanging onto the past, that's when I move forward. Recovering from the flood wasn't the worst blow I've suffered, and I was already in a state of shell shock from losing both of my parents when the flood hit.

Just because I was "over it," didn't mean that I didn't have to deal with adjustment, but I was ready to shed the baggage of flood survivor. There were a myriad of nuisances, like not having proper clothes for a funeral. I can't tell you how many invitations I turned down for lack of something appropriate to wear.

You have no idea how long it takes to stock a kitchen until you have to do it. For the first year, every time I tried to cook, I was missing some of the ingredients, or I didn't have the proper small appliances. Those types of nuisances were endless, but slowly, you begin to replace things and life becomes easier. In the beginning, I felt like a frontier woman, but with each replaced lost item, life became easier.

I know the lessons I learned during and after the flood helped my transition back to a normal life. I'm sure they will come in handy in the future. I'm grateful for the lessons, but I could have done without the flood to learn them. They say that you repeat lessons until you learn them. Maybe that was the purpose of the flood—the lessons learned.

If you can apply some of the lessons we three have taken away from our waves of change, then we've succeeded in getting our story out. If we have nudged you into preparing for and surviving both physically and emotionally from some future disaster, we have done our job. Whatever lies ahead, we all have coping mechanisms within us to help us get beyond the moment no matter how it may seem at the time. It's up to us to draw on those resources.

Before the flood, I had stubbornly refused help most of my life. This life-changing experience helped me learn how to accept the gifts that flowed my way, and by putting my stubbornness aside, I was able to recover relatively quickly and easily (emphasis on the word "relatively").

It is our sincerest hope that the next time you find yourself in the eye of the storm you will find your own perfect way to weather the storm until the sun shines again—as it always does.

APPENDIX

Holmes and Rahe Stress Scale

The Holmes and Rahe Stress Scale measures the number of changes/transitions in a one-year period. Remember that change impacts our psyche, upsets our equilibrium, and can put our bodies and minds into a state of shock. Left unprocessed, the shock settles into us. We need to acknowledge the changes that are going on in our lives. Our coping skills, resiliency, and immune system are all compromised when we don't take time to regroup. That is, we must pause, evaluate, adjust, plan, and heal. Take a moment to see where you fall on the scale. Then, periodically recheck yourself. Remember information can give us an offensive vs. defensive position and allow us to act vs. react.

Holmes and Rahe Stress Scale
Multiply each event by the number of times you have experienced it in the last year.

	Life Event (Stressor)	Value	#/Yr	=	Total
1.	Death of spouse	100 X	____	=	____
2.	Divorce	73 X	____	=	____
3.	Jail time	63 X	____	=	____
4.	Death of a close family member	63 X	____	=	____
5.	Major personal injury or illness	53 X	1	=	53
6.	Marriage	50 X	____	=	____
7.	Fired from work	47 X	____	=	____
8.	Marital reconciliation	45 X	____	=	____
9.	Retirement	45 X	____	=	____
10.	Major change in health of family member	44 X	3	=	132
11.	Pregnancy	40 X	____	=	____
12.	Sex difficulties	39 X	____	=	____
13.	Gain of new family member	39 X	2	=	78
14.	Major business readjustment	39 X	1	=	39
15.	Major change in financial state	38 X	1	=	38
16.	Death of close friend	37 X	____	=	____
17.	Change to different line of work	36 X	____	=	____
18.	Major change in number of arguments with spouse	35 X	____	=	____
19.	Mortgage over $100,000	31 X	____	=	____
20.	Foreclosure of mortgage or loan	30 X	____	=	____
21.	Major change in responsibilities at work	29 X	____	=	____
22.	Son or daughter leaving home	29 X	____	=	____
23.	Trouble with in-laws	29 X	____	=	____
24.	Outstanding personal achievement	28 X	____	=	____

Appendix

25.	Spouse begins or stops job	27 X	2	=	54
26.	Begin or end school	26 X	___	=	___
27.	Major change in living conditions	25 X	___	=	___
28.	Revision of personal habits	24 X	1	=	24
29.	Trouble with boss	23 X	___	=	___
30.	Major change in work hours or conditions	20 X	___	=	___
31.	Change in residence or schools	20 X	___	=	___
32.	Major change in recreation	19 X	___	=	___
33.	Major change in church activities	19 X	1	=	19
34.	Major change in social activities	18 X	1	=	18
35.	Mortgage or loan less than $10,000	17 X	4	=	68
36.	Major change in sleeping habits	16 X	___	=	___
37.	Major change in number of family get-togethers	15 X	___	=	___
38.	Major change in eating habits	15 X	___	=	___
39.	Vacations, Christmas	13 X	1	=	___
40.	Minor violations of the law	11 X	___	=	___

Total Score 523

Scoring the Holmes and Rahe Stress Scale

Holmes and Rahe found that a score of 150 gives you a 50-50 chance of developing an illness. A score of 300+ gives you a 90 percent chance of developing an illness, having an accident, or "blowing up." Notice that "positive times" like Christmas, marriage, and vacations are stressful.

Personality Type Stress Susceptibility Test

Type A personalities tend to be more susceptible to stress. They typically take on too much. They often struggle to say "no" either because they are good at everything, can't delegate because "no one does it the 'right' way," hide in their workaholism, or have become accustomed to a hyper-busy state of existence where off-the-charts busy is just the norm. If you have a Type A personality, chances are you already know it. On the other hand, perhaps you've been too busy to notice that you are stressed! Take a moment to see how susceptible you are to stress.

Personality Type Stress Susceptibility Test
Use the number scale to indicate how strongly you feel about each statement below:

5 – Always happens
4 – Almost always happens
3 – Sometimes happens
2 – Rarely happens
1 – Never happens

1. Other people often remark about how fast I move, walk, talk, and/or eat.   _3_
2. I become irritated, even enraged, when driving behind a vehicle that is moving too slowly.   _2_
3. I become irritated when I have to wait in lines at banks, post offices, stores.   _1_
4. I feel impatient with the rate at which most things take place.   _4_
5. I become impatient when doing repetitive work such as washing dishes, mailing envelopes, filling out forms, etc.   _2_
6. I often find myself trying to do two or more   _2_

Appendix

things at the same time.
7. I feel guilty relaxing or just doing nothing for a few hours. _3_
8. I find myself constantly evaluating things in terms of numbers, breaking things down into hours, minutes, seconds, or into dollars and cents. _1_
9. I often challenge those ahead of me in traffic or doing a similar activity. _1_
10. I often find myself scheduling more and more into less and less time. _2_

Total Score: _18_

10–19 Low   **20–31 Medium**   **32–50 High**

Key: The higher you score the more "Type A" you are and the more susceptible you are to stress.

Address Stress with Success Test

It's important to manage your life with intention, and to regularly evaluate what you allow into your life and what you put into your mind and body. The Address Stress with Success Test is another quick way to identify areas in which you might want to make changes to improve your ability to address stress. Sometimes we forget how closely intertwined our physical, emotional, mental, social, and spiritual components really are. When one or more components are "out of whack," the others are indirectly impacted negatively. Conversely, when there is strength in one or more components, the others are indirectly positively impacted.

Address Stress with Success Test
Use the number scale to indicate how strongly you feel about each statement below:

5 – Always
4 – Almost always
3 – Sometimes
2 – Rarely
1 – Never

1. I exercise at least 30 minutes, three times a week. 4
2. I average between seven to eight hours of sleep every night. 5
3. I have a consistent job/work schedule. 3
4. I have a consistent nighttime sleep pattern. 5
5. I feel good about my present job situation. 2
6. I have a regular meal schedule. 5
7. I am in good overall health. 4
8. I plan, organize, and use my time effectively. 3
9. I feel good about the relationship I have with 3

Appendix

	my significant other.	
10.	I drink less than five alcoholic beverages per week.	5
11.	I avoid smoking cigarettes.	5
12.	I avoid the use of any form of drugs.	5
13.	I limit the amount of coffee and sodas I drink.	5
14.	I have several close friends with whom I can talk about personal problems.	4
15.	I am able to live on less than I earn.	2
16.	I have a sense of purpose and direction in life.	3
17.	I am at the right approximate weight for my height.	4
18.	I try to eat a healthy diet avoiding foods high in fat and carbs.	5
19.	I receive strength from my spiritual beliefs.	5
20.	I regularly set aside personal time to have fun and enjoy my hobbies.	4

Total Score 81

85–100: Excellent
70–84: Good
Below 70: Improvement Needed

100 Stress Busters

Dosage: Use one a day for 100 days. If stress persists, continue using until symptoms subside. For more immediate results, try two or more a day.

1. Get up earlier. If you're not a morning person, good luck!
2. Make repairs. But hey, if it's not broken, don't fix it.
3. Take a bubble bath. Don't swallow the bubbles; you know what that does.
4. Go fly a kite. That's right, just do it. And take a kid with you to teach.
5. Be aware of your decisions, and be decisive about your awareness.
6. Start a joy file. Anything funny, heartwarming, and special goes in a file for those joyless days.
7. Walk in the rain. Even better—sing in the rain.
8. Whistle or hum a tune (a happy one).
9. Hold a baby. If it isn't yours, give it back to its rightful owner.
10. Unclutter your life. Maybe start with your closets and drawers.
11. Say "no" if you don't really want to say "yes."
12. Say "no" to drugs. They may appear to manage stress, but they actually create more.
13. Quit trying to fix others, and work on yourself instead. Like they say in AA, "Get out of their lives and into your own."
14. Get enough sleep. Sleeping Beauty did and you know how that story ended.
15. Build a support network. Start by strengthening or building one meaningful friendship.
16. Breathe slowly, but don't stop altogether. Practice slow, purposeful breathing.

Appendix

17. Decide it's more important to get along than to be right.
18. Learn a joke. Then, try to tell it like your favorite comedian would.
19. Say, "Have a good day," in pig Latin.
20. Meet your limits. Then exceed them.
21. Make and throw a paper airplane, but don't crash it into someone's face.
22. Eat a meal by candlelight.
23. Go on a picnic, or have one on the floor at home. Just as fun and no pesky ants.
24. Watch one of your favorite movies and eat popcorn—with butter and salt. Just for today, eat it the way you really like it.
25. Talk less and listen more. We have two ears and one mouth. You do the math!
26. Praise and encourage someone. Start with yourself first.
27. Remember you always have choices and options.
28. Put an air freshener in your car, preferably one that doesn't make you nauseated.
29. Drive a different route to work. Make sure you still know how to get there.
30. Learn a new song. Then, sing it at the top of your lungs. If you have a bad voice, perhaps singing within the habitat of your shower or car would be wise.
31. Leave work early. If you feel extra naughty and won't lose your job, don't tell anyone you're leaving.
32. Write to a faraway friend. Then plan a trip to go see your friend. If on a budget, invite your friend to come and visit you.
33. Scream at a ball game. If it's your kids' game, this can really irritate them, but hey, you know your kids. If they won't hate you afterward, go for it!
34. Write in a journal. If you don't have one, write in someone else's. Just kidding. Just write your thoughts and feelings on a piece of paper. That works too.

35. Smile. It takes fewer muscles than a frown and often is the precursor to laughter.
36. Listen to a symphony, or if you play an instrument, play your own.
37. Read a poem, or better yet, write one.
38. Watch a ballet. Can't do that? Pretend you're a prima ballerina and pirouette across your living room unashamedly.
39. Do something you've never done before. Make sure it's legal.
40. Buy some flowers and smell them. Pick some if you prefer. If you pick them from the neighbor's yard, make sure you are friends. If you're not friends, make sure they don't see you.
41. Say hello to a stranger. This may be against some cultural norms. Oh well, do it anyway.
42. Stop a bad habit. Or if you prefer, start a good one. Or if you are feeling super assertive, do both, but by all means, do not start a bad habit and stop a good one.
43. Don't have to know all the answers. You'll be wrong for sure anyway.
44. Schedule time to do nothing—absolutely nothing. You might have to start small and build up the time spent doing nothing if you are completely unfamiliar with the concept of chillaxing.
45. Stop negative talk—both to others and to yourself.
46. Read a story. Pretend you are the main character unless you don't like that one. In that case, pick another character to understudy.
47. Stretch your limits. And for added benefit, stretch your quadriceps as well.
48. Look at a favorite piece of art. If you don't have it framed on your wall, look it up in a book or online. Then, make plans to buy it.
49. Plant a tree.

Appendix

50. Feed the birds. Try the ducks at a park, or a bird feeder in the backyard. It's all good. Don't have a bird feeder? Make plans to get one. They're cheap at Home Depot or Lowe's.
51. Ask a friend for a hug. Everybody likes hugs.
52. Look for the silver lining. Every cloud has one. It's a proven fact.
53. Make a decision you have been putting off. See how much better you feel? Can't make the decision today? Recognize that at least you are one day closer to making it.
54. Simplify meals. There's something to be said for fruit and cheese or steamed veggies smothered with melted cheese. It's entirely possible that two out of the four basic food groups aren't good for you anyway.
55. For some extra fun have a "backwards meal." Eat under the table, use spatulas for silverware and cookie sheets for plates. Aawww, come on, just try it!
56. Go for excellence, not perfection. Excellence is achievable; perfection is not.
57. Practice unconditional love, you know the kind where you just give it without expecting to get something back.
58. Pet a dog or cat. Remember not to pet the sweaty stuff and don't sweat the petty stuff either.
59. Make an appointment for something you have been putting off.
60. Laugh, laugh, just laugh. It really is true. It's the best medicine.
61. Visualize winning. It's half the battle. Remember too that even if you don't win, you still are a winner just for being in and staying in the game.
62. Work on your sense of humor. Remember what they say: "Don't take yourself too seriously."

63. Get some sidewalk chalk and play hopscotch. Remember how much fun you used to have in second grade? It's almost as fun, just harder, to bend down and pick up that crazy token you throw into the square.
64. Get help with a job or project you have been putting off because you don't want to do it or don't know how.
65. Along those same lines, break down a large task into small pieces. That way you can feel good about accomplishing part of it or, at least, feel more positive about it.
66. Take a drive. If it can be along the coast, great. If not, pretend you smell the ocean.
67. Look at the stars and ponder how small you are in the overall scheme of things but how big you are to God anyway.
68. Practice preventative maintenance, whatever that means. It's a very individual thing; you'll know what it means to you.
69. Make duplicate keys. Remember that time you locked yourself out of the house or the car? Wasn't fun, was it? Ok, so let's not do that again.
70. Use your time wisely, and be timely about using your wisdom.
71. Play with a child.
72. Clean up a mess—that one you have been avoiding.
73. Put on a relaxation tape and pretend you are in a yoga class. Or go to a yoga class. It's a good bet they have their own relaxation tape there.
74. Say hello to that person you always see and never say hello to. You might just make their day and your own at the same time.
75. Prepare for an emergency, so you will feel more in control of an uncontrollable event.
76. Get rid of anything that isn't useful, beautiful, or joyful. That covers a lot of ground.

Appendix

77. Ponder the fact that everything can change in the blink of an eye but that God never changes and never blinks.
78. Forgive. But remember, forgiveness is a process that starts with the decision to be willing to forgive. Sometimes we even have to start with the decision to be willing to be willing.
79. Frame every so-called disaster with this question: "In ten days, ten weeks, ten years… will this matter?"
80. Remember that what others think of you is really none of your business. What do you think of you? Decide today to focus on what you like about yourself. That is your business.
81. Don't audit life. Get up, dress up, and show up.
82. Pay off part of your credit card today. You'll be a step closer to being free of that killer interest rate.
83. Expect a miracle today. They are just waiting to happen all the time. You have to look for them.
84. Yield. Give up the right of way. See what happens.
85. Make peace with your past, so it won't mess up your present and future.
86. Your job won't take care of you when you are sick. Your friends and family will. Keep your priorities straight.
87. Think of God often today, and tell Him about it.
88. Use all five senses today to take in all you can of the day. What do you see, hear, feel, touch, taste?
89. Get outside today. Nature is amazing. Sometimes we are too busy and we miss it. Don't miss it today!
90. Make a gratitude list before you go to sleep. Think of five things you are grateful for today and every day. This could actually be a good practice every night.
91. Say a prayer today. Instead of asking God for something, maybe thank Him for what you already have.
92. Eat something healthy instead of junk. Savor the natural taste.

93. Schedule a getaway weekend, or day, or hour.
94. Believe you can do it, whatever it is.
95. Practice grace and mercy. Test it out on yourself first. We really are pretty hard on ourselves.
96. Work on losing weight to be healthier and feel better, not just to get into those tight jeans. Don't let the scale determine how you feel about yourself. Can't get around that? Set it lower by five pounds and then forget you changed it. You will be really impressed with yourself.
97. Get in to work early and finish early. Then do something nice to reward yourself for finishing early.
98. Sit in the sunshine. Feel the warmth soak in. No sun where you live? Be grateful you have something to look forward to. It will be sunny in a few months.
99. Treat yourself to a massage, or get the poor man's version of one. Ask a family member to rub some lotion on your feet and hands. Warning: you may have to pay them.
100. Take each day one at a time; you have the rest of your life to LIVE each of them.

R.I.P. Miss Fluff

Visit us at

www.waves-of-change.net

and

facebook.com/wavesofchangetn

ABOUT THE AUTHORS

Pamala Hernandez-Kaufman, LMFT, is a bilingual licensed marriage and family therapist with 14 years of experience working with individuals, couples, adolescents, and children in English and Spanish. Most of her work is with PTSD, grief, loss, and trauma recovery, and she deploys regularly for crisis intervention and disaster relief work. Her private practice office is in Brentwood, Tenn.

MJ Plaster has been a technical writer, instructional designer, instructor, speaker, and freelance writer for more decades than she would like recall, with newspaper, magazine, anthology, corporate, online, and agency writing to her credit. In addition to writing, she has served as managing editor for several association and special publications, including the *Florida Turf Digest* since 2006.

Melissa Riley, Ph.D., WEMT-IV, is the state coordinator for the Tennessee Disaster Crisis Counseling Program. She volunteers as the K9 coordinator for Tennessee Task Force 2 State Urban Search and Rescue Team (USAR), the Wilson County Sheriff K9 Search and Rescue Team, and as the technical rescue coordinator for the Wilson County Disaster Animal Response Team (DART). She is a flight instructor, a FEMA CCP Instructor, and instructs for the University of Phoenix. She is also a wilderness emergency medical technician, firefighter, emergency planner, and has over two decades of experience in emergency services as a responder and an instructor.

Made in the USA
Charleston, SC
15 January 2016